Towel +
Cold Noodles
てぬぐい+冷たい麺

➡P124,P194

Chukagai

中華街

➡P160

hide88 / PIXTA（ピクスタ）

B-Class Gourmet
B級グルメ

Photo: ささざわ / PIXTA（ピクスタ）

➡P210

Manekineko
招き猫

➡P028

Dagashiya
駄菓子屋

➡P010

Industrial Zones

工業地帯

➡️P246

Photo: Lin / PIXTA(ピクスタ)

Parking in a Parking Lot

駐車場での停め方

Photo: yamahide / PIXTA（ピクスタ）

➡P152

Illumination
イルミネーション

➡P053

和食や日本のカルチャーは、いまや世界規模で大流行しています。ガイドブックを開けば、世界遺産をはじめとする日本の有名な観光名所や、おすすめレストランについての記述がずらり。世界中の人が「日本通」だといってもいいかもしれません。

でも、実は海外からの観光客が本当に知りたいのは、そんな有名な観光スポットや定番のグルメだけでなく、日本の「今」がわかるリアルなカルチャーや暮らし、食だったりします。つまりそれは、日本のみなさんが当たり前のように暮らしている「日常そのもの」。

そこで、今回はあえて、ガイドブックではあまり取り上げていない、日本に根差した生活習慣や食事スタイル、文化などについて紹介しています。私が日本で暮らすうちに気づいた、興味深い日本の習慣や行動のほか、いま話題のトピックスについてもピックアップしてみました。

「都市伝説」や「田舎暮らし」、「せんべろ」……皆さんならどう説明しますか？

すべてのトピックスは会話形式の Q&A になっていて、実践の場で、即使いやすいつくりになっています。きっと外国の方との雑談もはずみ、心の距離もぐっと縮まることでしょう（私が日本に来たばかりのころ、こんなに明快＆簡潔に日本文化を紹介してもらえたら、どんなにうれしかったことか！という気持ちもこめました）。

私の知識のおよぶ範囲で、できるだけ詳しく説明したつもりですが、ここにあなたならではの経験や知識をプラスし、さらに濃厚でオリジナリティあふれるガイドブックに仕上げていただければ幸いです。

最後に、本書の執筆にあたり、さまざまなご提案やご協力をいただいた、Ｊリサーチ出版の新谷祥子さんに、この場を借りてお礼申し上げます。

Let's rediscover the beauty and wonder of Japan and share it with the world!

デイビッド・セイン

CONTENTS

Chapter 2

外国人がいちばん不思議に思う
日本のくらし・習慣

Chapter 3

外国人がいちばん不思議に思う
日本の食文化 185

Chapter 4

外国人がいちばん不思議に思う
日本の娯楽・建造物・宿泊.........................231

How to use this book
本書の利用法

本書は全4章構成で、1テーマにつき2ないし3ページで、
簡単な英語で日本のカルチャーやくらしを案内しています。

ここで学ぶテーマです。

無料音声ダウンロードの
ファイル番号です。

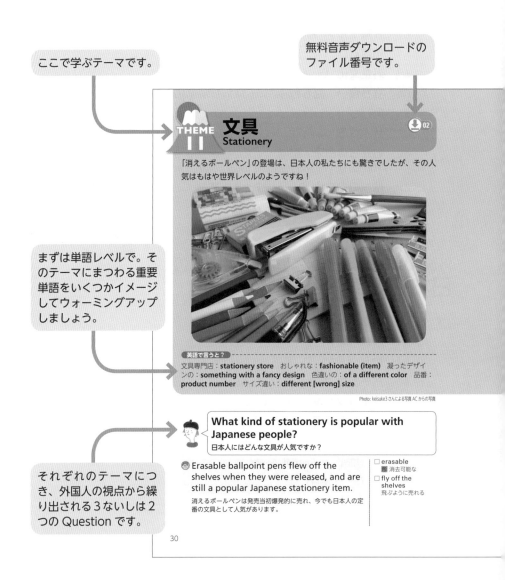

THEME 11 文具
Stationery

(↓02)

「消えるボールペン」の登場は、日本人の私たちにも驚きでしたが、その人気はもはや世界レベルのようですね！

まずは単語レベルで。そのテーマにまつわる重要単語をいくつかイメージしてウォーミングアップしましょう。

英語で言うと？
文具専門店：**stationery store**　おしゃれな：**fashionable (item)**　凝ったデザインの：**something with a fancy design**　色違いの：**of a different color**　品番：**product number**　サイズ違い：**different [wrong] size**

Photo: keisuke3 さんによる写真 AC からの写真

それぞれのテーマにつき、外国人の視点から繰り出される3ないしは2つの Question です。

What kind of stationery is popular with Japanese people?
日本人にはどんな文具が人気ですか？

Erasable ballpoint pens flew off the shelves when they were released, and are still a popular Japanese stationery item.
消えるボールペンは発売当初爆発的に売れ、今でも日本人の定番の文具として人気があります。

☐ erasable
消去可能な
☐ fly off the shelves
飛ぶように売れる

30

Question に簡単な英語で答えていきます。基本的には3ステップで説明していきます。中学レベルのシンプルな英語で、[概論⇒説明⇒おすすめポイントや具体例など]という流れになっています。

文化

□ role 名 役：役割
□ promotion
名 販売促進

重要語句の品詞と意味です。

💬 Masking tape that you can write on is popular among women, and it's used for wrapping presents, decorating photo albums, and sticking to foods in the freezer.

女性の間では字が書けるマスキングテープが人気で、プレゼントのラッピングに使ったり、アルバムのデコレーション、冷凍庫に入れる食品に貼ったりします。

💬 Stickers are popular among girls, and you can collect them and exchange them with your friends. A sticker book for collecting stickers is also a popular item.

女の子にはシールが人気で、シールを集めたり、友達と交換して楽しみます。シールを貼るシール帳も人気のアイテムです。

 Where can I buy stationery?
文房具はどこで買えますか？

□ specialty
名 得意分野：特殊性

💬 You can buy it at specialty stationery stores. There are large ones with many types.

専門の文房具店で買えます。たくさんの種類を揃えた大型のものから、

💬 Bookstores and convenience stores also sell stationery. There is a stationery corner in department stores.

本屋やコンビニでも文房具を扱っています。デパートなどでも文房具コーナーがあります。

💬 You can buy stationery at a stationery-themed cafe.

文房具カフェという、文房具をテーマにしたカフェでもちょっと変わった文房具を買うことができます。

💡 毎年新たな文具の新製品が世に出てきます。実用的で (practical)、画期的な (breakthrough) ものがたくさん！

要所要所でそのテーマに関する＋αの情報や英語表現を収録しました。

31

7

音声・ダウンロードについて

【ダウンロード音声の内容】

★ Chapter 1 〜 4 すべての Question と Answer が、英語で収録されています。耳と口を鍛えて、実践力をアップしましょう!

【かんたん! 音声ダウンロードの手順】

STEP1 インターネットで
「https://audiobook.jp/exchange/jresearch」にアクセス!

※「J リサーチ出版のホームページ」(http://www.jresearch.co.jp) にある「音声ダウンロード」のバナーをクリックしていただくか、上記のURLを入力するか、右上のQRコードを使用してください。

STEP2 表示されたページから、audiobook.jpへの会員登録ページへ。

※音声のダウンロードには、オーディオブック配信サービス audiobook.jp への会員登録(無料)が必要です。すでに、audiobook.jp の会員の方は STEP 3 へお進みください。

STEP3 登録後、再度 STEP1 のページにアクセスし、シリアルコードの入力欄に「24604」を入力後、「送信」をクリック!

※作品がライブラリに追加されたと案内が出ます。

STEP4 必要な音声ファイルをダウンロード!

※スマートフォンの場合は、アプリ「audiobook.jp」の案内が出ますので、アプリからご利用ください。
※PCの場合は、「ライブラリ」から音声ファイルをダウンロードしてご利用ください。

〈ご注意!〉

● PCからでも、iPhone や Android のスマートフォンやタブレットからでも音声を再生いただけます。

● 音声は何度でもダウンロード・再生いただくことができます。

● ダウンロード・アプリについてのお問い合わせ先:
info@febe.jp (受付時間:平日の10時〜20時)

Chapter 1

外国人がいちばん不思議に思う
日本の文化

駐菓子から始まり妖怪、お化け、ラブホにイルミに温泉旅館まで、外国人が「？？？」と不思議に思う38のジャパニーズ・カルチャーを、ギュギュっと詰め込みました！

CULTURE

駄菓子屋
Dagashiya

01

究極のプチプライスみやげをご案内するならここ！　自分が子供時代に好きだった駄菓子について、英語で言う準備から始めてみましょう！

気分はもはや宝探し！

英語で言うと？ -

麩菓子：**wheat gluten snack**　麦チョコ：**chocolate-covered barley puffs**　酢コンブ：**vinegared kelp**　のしいか：**flattened dried squid**　ラムネ：**lemon-lime soda**　ポン菓子：**puffed cereal**

What sort of place is a *dagashiya*?
駄菓子屋とはどんなところですか？

● It's a comparatively small store that sells snacks called *dagashi*.

☐ comparatively
副 比較的

駄菓子と呼ばれるお菓子を売っている、比較的小規模なお店のことです。

● Elementary and junior high school students in the area buy snacks there on the way home.

☐ elementary
形 初等の

その地域の小学生や中学生が学校の帰りなどに寄っておやつを買ったりします。

🙂 Some of them sell toys and provide light meals.

□ light meal　軽食

おもちゃを売っていたり、軽食を提供するお店もあります。

What are *dagashi*?
駄菓子って何？

🙂 They're cheap snacks for kids.

子供向けの安いお菓子のことです。

🙂 You can usually buy them for ten to one hundred yen.

たいてい10円〜100円以内で購入できます。

🙂 Snacks that come with prizes or toys are also popular.

□ prize　名 景品

くじやおもちゃなどのおまけ付きのお菓子も人気があります。

Can you buy *dagashi* outside of *dagashiya*?
駄菓子屋以外でも駄菓子は買えますか？

🙂 You can sometimes buy them at department stores and large supermarkets.

百貨店や大型スーパーなどに駄菓子店舗が入っていることがあります。

🙂 Some convenience stores also have *dagashi*.

コンビニでも駄菓子を扱う店舗があります。

🙂 You can also buy them at hundred yen shops.

100円ショップでも買うことができます。

💬 ほかにも、「3時の時おやつ」の代表格であった「カステラ」は sponge cake、縁日などでおなじみの「わたあめ」は cotton candy で表せます。

11

プリントシール機
Sticker Printing Machines

⬇ 02

今やスマートフォンを使えば写真はいくらでも撮れますが、日本の「ゲーセン」でのプリントシール撮影体験は、いい旅行の思い出になるはず！

英語で言うと？

背景：**background**　フレーム：**frame**　ゲーセン：**arcade**　女子高生：**female high-school student**　修正する：**modify**　大きくする：**enlarge**

What's a sticker printing machine?
プリントシール機ってなんですか？

It's a machine that takes a picture of your face or body with a camera and prints a photo on a sticker.

自分の顔や全身をカメラで撮影し、シールに印刷された写真が出てくる機械です。

You can choose from many types of backgrounds and frames.

◉ よく聞く「プリクラ」は、セガホールディングスの登録商標（registered trade mark）です。

□ background
　名 背景

□ frame　名 枠；額縁

背景やフレームなどたくさんの種類から選ぶことができます。

💬 Nowadays, many people send images to their mobile phones and save them rather than printing them on stickers.

最近ではシールに印刷するよりも、自分の携帯に画像を送って保存する人が多いです。

What can you do with the machine?
どんなことができるの？

💬 There are functions to enlarge the eyes, make the face smaller, modify the face, and make the legs thinner.

目を大きくしたり、顔を小さくしたり、顔の修正をしたり…脚を細くする機能もあります。

☐ enlarge
動 ～を大きくする
☐ modify
動 修正する
☐ thin
形 薄い；やせた

💬 You can also use a tablet to enter your own handwritten text. You can also put stamps on the photo.

タブレットを使って、自分たちの手書きの文字を入れることもできます。スタンプなどを押すこともできます。

☐ handwritten
形 手書きの

💬 Some machines can print a photo like it was taken in a two-shot with a celebrity.

有名人とツーショットを撮ったようにできるものもあります。

Where can I take the photos?
どこで撮れるの？

💬 You can take photos at many arcades. Some floors have nothing but sticker printing machines.

多くのゲームセンターで撮ることができます。プリントシール機だけが置かれているフロアがあるところもあります。

☐ arcade
名 ゲームセンター

💬 Some large shopping malls, sightseeing spots and amusement parks have sticker printing machines installed.

大型モール店や観光地やアミューズメントパークでもプリントシール機が設置してあるところがあります。

☐ sightseeing spot
観光地

文化

THEME 3 JK文化
JK Culture

ルーズソックス、タピオカ、プリ…日本の女子高生による独特の文化は、さまざまなジャンルでブームを巻き起こすほどエネルギッシュ！

高校生の部活や生活をテーマにした漫画や映画作品も要チェック！

英語で言うと？ --

ルーズソックス：**baggy socks** タピオカ：**tapioca** ブーム：**trend** 移り変わりが激しい：**drastic change** マーケティング：**marketing** おしゃれな：**fashionable**

What does JK mean?
JKって何ですか？

It stands for the Japanese words "joshi" and "koukousei".

日本語の女子（Joshi）高校生（Koukousei）の頭文字をとったものです。

It means a Japanese high school girl.

日本の女子高校生を指します。

□ stand for （略語などが）～を表す

14

🙂 We also call middle school girls JC, elementary school girls JS, and female university students JD.

女子中学生はJC、女子小学生はJS、女子大生はJDと略すことも あります。

☐ middle school
中学校

What characteristics do they have?
どんな特徴があるのですか？

🙂 There are words specific to high school girls that they use in conversation and on social media, and most of them are hard for adults to understand.

女子高生特有の言葉が存在し、会話やSNSのやり取りで使用さ れ、大人には理解するのが難しいものがほとんどです。

☐ specific
形 特有の；明確な
☐ social media
ソーシャルメディア

🙂 A lot of trends are started by high school girls.

女子高生から火がつくブームがたくさんあります。

🙂 There are things like fashion and make-up styles that are unique to high school girls.

ファッションやメイクなども女子高生独自のものが存在します。

☐ unique to
～に特有の

What kind of trends were there in the past?
これまでにどんなブームがありましたか？

🙂 An old one is the trend of loose socks that was said to have started with high school girls.

古くはルーズソックスは女子高生から始まったとされています。

☐ loose socks
ルーズソックス

🙂 Printed stickers are another item that evolved thanks to high school girls.

プリントシール機も女子高生により進化したものの一つです。

☐ evolve
動 発展［進化］する

🙂 Food and drink trends like tapioca are said to be transmitted by high school girls.

タピオカなど飲食のブームも、女子高生から発信されることが あります。

☐ transmit
動 発信する

文
化

THEME 4

サバイバルゲーム
Survival Game

📥 04

サバゲーというと、森の中で迷彩服を着て撃ち合うイメージですが、最近では都心部に完全インドアのフィールドもあり、気軽にトライできます。

英語で言うと？ -

BB弾：**BB pellets**　環境にやさしい：**environmentally friendly**
迷彩服：**camouflage clothing**　装備：**equipment**　エアソフトガン：**air gun**
都市部：**urban area**

Photo: けーすけ ans さんによる写真ACからの写真

What's a survival game?
サバイバルゲームって何ですか？

💬 It's a game with elements of sport where the players are divided into teams, and is played indoors or outdoors.

敵味方に分かれて、野外および屋内で行われるスポーツ要素のあるゲームです。

💬 It's played wearing clothes that are easy to move in, with a helmet and goggles on.

☐ element　名 要素
☐ divide into
　　～に分かれる

動きやすい服装で、ヘルメットやゴーグルなどを装備して行われます。

🗣 Sometimes it's shortened to "sabagē" or "sabage".

「サバゲー」や「サバゲ」と略させれることもあります。

□ shorten
動 短くする

What do you do in this game?
どんなことをするゲームですか？

🗣 You shoot BB pellets at each other with a toy gun called an "airsoft gun".

エアソフトガンと呼ばれるおもちゃの銃でBB弾を撃ち合います。

□ pellet
名 (散弾銃や空気銃の) ペレット

🗣 There are BB pellets made of plastic, and those made of environmentally-friendly materials.

BB弾はプラスチック製のものや、環境に優しい素材でできているものがあります。

□ environmentally-friendly
環境にやさしい

🗣 Basically, if you get shot by an enemy, you lose. The team with the most remaining members at the end wins.

基本的に、敵に打たれたらその人は負けです。最終的な生存人数の多さを競います。

□ get shot
銃で撃たれる
□ lose 動 負ける
□ remaining
形 残っている

Where can I try it?
どこで体験できますか？

🗣 You can mainly try it at special venues called "sabagē fields".

主に「サバゲーフィールド」と呼ばれる、専用の場所で体験することができます。

□ mainly 副 主に
□ venue 名 開催地

➲ 屋外型のサバゲーフィールドは都市部より郊外 (suburb) に多いです。

🗣 There's a fee of about 3,000 to 5,000 yen per person.

料金はだいたい1人3,000〜5,000円ぐらいです。

🗣 If you search online you can find them all over Japan.

ネットなどで検索すれば日本各地で見つけることができます。

THEME 5 脱出ゲーム
Escape Room

05

パソコンやスマホで遊べる「脱出ゲーム」も楽しいですが、せっかくなら実際の施設に足を運んで「脱出」をフィジカルに体験してみましょう！

徳島県にあるイルローザの森の迷路。大人も子供も楽しめる！

英語で言うと？

謎解き：**solve riddles**　巨大迷路：**giant maze**　廃校［病院］：**abandoned school [hospital]**　期間限定：**limited edition**　特設会場：**special venue**

Photo: haku-さんによる写真ACからの写真

What's an escape room?
脱出ゲームとはどんなゲームですか？

It's a reality game where you solve riddles to escape from a locked room.

謎解きなどをしながら、閉鎖された空間から脱出する体感型のゲームです。

There are puzzles and games as well as riddles, and some of them have time limits.

☐ reality　名 現実性
☐ solve　動 解決する
☐ riddle　名 謎

18

謎解きのほかにも、パズルやゲームなどがあり、時間制限を設けたものもあります。

🙂 There are lots of different themes, like detective and horror.

探偵ものやホラーなど、テーマは様々です。

Where can I try it?
どんな場所で体験できるのですか？

🙂 They're set up as attractions at theme parks and amusement parks.

遊園地やアミューズメントパーク内のアトラクションとして設けられています。

🙂 Some also use real places like abandoned schools or hospitals.

廃校や廃病院が使われる本格的な場所もあります。

🙂 Some are held for a limited time in special venues during times like summer vacation.

夏休みなどの期間限定で、 特設会場で行われることもあります。

Are there also rooms that can be enjoyed by children?
子供でも楽しめるものはありますか？

🙂 In that case, I would recommend a giant maze.

それなら巨大迷路がおすすめです。

🙂 They are safe, as there are doors along the way in case a child wants to stop partway through.

途中でリタイアするためのトビラがついているので安心です。

🙂 Recently, there are three-dimensional mazes where you can also move upward and downward!

最近では、上下にも移動する立体迷路なんていうのもあります！

文化

THEME 6 血液型にやたらこだわる

Caring about Blood Types

 06

日本人の雑談トピックの TOP10 には絶対入ってくると思われる「血液型」。
性格を表す形容詞をいろいろ取りそろえると話が膨らむかも！

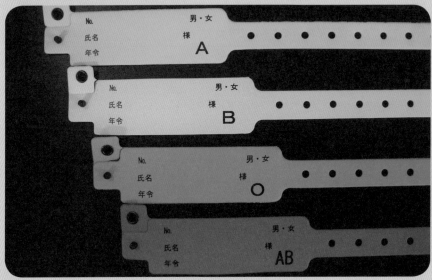

日本人は誰でも一度は「何型何型?」と聞かれた経験アリ！

英語で言うと？

几帳面な：**well-organized pace** 大らかな：**laid back** マイペースな：**at one's own**
敏感な：**perceptive** 鈍感な：**insensitive** 勤勉な：**diligent**

Why do Japanese people care about blood type so much?

日本人はどうして血液型にこだわるのですか？

😊 Lots of people believe in blood type horoscopes.

血液型占いというものの存在が大きいです。

😊 These horoscopes divide people into personalities based on blood types.

☐ horoscope
　名 占い

☐ divide
　動 〜を分ける

☐ personality
　名 性格；人格

☐ based on
　〜に基づいて

その占いでは血液型ごとに性格が分類されています。

 It was once a fad on TV and in books, so lots of people started to believe in those qualities.

一時期テレビや本などでブームとなったことで、その性質を多くの人が信じるようになりました。

□ fad 名 一時的流行

文化

How are people generally classified?

大まかにどんな風に分類されているの？

 A-type is the most common in Japan, and those people are said to be serious and well-organized.

A型は日本人に一番多く、真面目で几帳面とされています。

 O-type is the second most common, and those people are said to be easy-going.

O型はその次に多く、おおらかな性格とされています。

B-types take things at their own pace, and AB-types are said to have two sides.

B型はマイペース、AB型は二面性があるとされています。

□ classify
　動 ～を分類する

□ said to be
　～だと言われている

□ well-organized
　几帳面な

□ easy-going
　のんきな

□ at one's own
　pace　マイペースで

How does this affect people's lives?

生活にはどんな風に影響していますか？

People check their compatibility in love and relationships.

恋愛や人間関係における相性をみたりします。

Some people have blood types they like and dislike.

人によって好きな血液型や嫌いな血液型がある人もいます。

In the past, there were also companies that hired based on blood type.

昔は血液型で採用を決める企業も存在しました。

□ affect
　動 ～に作用する

□ compatibility
　名 相性

□ relationship
　名 関係 (性)；恋愛関係

□ dislike
　動 ～を嫌う

□ hire　動 雇う

21

ラッピング
Gift Wrapping

 07

贈り物やお金を「裸」で渡すのをよしとしない日本人の考え方が根底にあることをお伝えできると、理解されやすいのではないでしょうか。

日本の「包むもの」といえば風呂敷。これもまた人気！

英語で言うと？ ---

包む：**wrap**　結ぶ：**tie**　包装紙：**wrapping paper**　リボン：**ribbon**
飾る：**decollate**　緩衝材：**packing material**

Photo: さつそらさんによる写真 AC からの写真

Why do you wrap gifts?
どうしてラッピングをするのですか？

It's said that the culture of wrapping gifts began with a cloth so that the gifts didn't get dirty.

包む文化は、お供え物が汚れないように敷物をしたことが始まりだと言われています。

□ wrap　動 〜を包む

🙂 There is the idea that it is rude to give things like gifts and cash with no wrapping.

贈り物、現金などを裸で渡すのは失礼だという考え方があります。

🙂 When you give a gift to a person, it makes it look good and shows respect to them.

人への贈り物をする時、見栄えをよくして相手への敬意を表します。

 Is wrapping free?
ラッピングは無料ですか？

🙂 There are free and paid ones.

無料のものと有料のものがあります。

🙂 If it's paid it's usually around 100 yen.

有料の場合は、大抵100円前後になります。

🙂 If you put it in a box, there are some that cost 200 to 500 yen or more.

箱をつけると200円から500円を超えるものもあります。

 What do you wrap gifts in?
どんなもので包むのですか？

🙂 We wrap them in paper with a color or pattern called wrapping paper.

包装紙と呼ばれる色や柄のついた紙で包みます。

🙂 In high-end stores, Japanese paper and cloth are sometimes used.

高級店などでは、和紙や布を使うこともあります。

🙂 A cushioning material may be used to prevent the product from being broken.

商品が壊れないように緩衝材を使うこともあります。

🍵 子供に渡す「おこづかい」はpocket moneyと言います。日本語の「ポケットマネー」とはちょっとニュアンスがちがいますね。

□ show respect
敬意を示す

🍵「化粧箱」は英語でvanity caseと言います。

□ pattern
　名 模様；図案
□ wrapping paper
　包装紙

□ high-end store
　高級店
□ Japanese paper
　和紙

□ cushioning
　material　緩衝材

文化

本の帯
Book *Obi*

📥 08

書店で売られている本についている帯、我々にはおなじみですが、そういう文化や価値観が全くない国のお客様もいらっしゃいます！

本の中身が気になる！

英語で言うと？

キャッチコピー：**advertising copy**　　有名人：**famous person**
しおり：**bookmark**　宣伝する：**publicize**　推薦コメント：**testimonial**
販売促進：**sales promotion**

Why do Japanese books have *obi*?
なぜ日本の本には帯が付いているのですか？

😊 They're for displaying advertising copy to sell the book.

その本を売るためのキャッチコピーを載せるためです。

😊 It's to make people who don't know what's in the book interested in it.

内容を知らない客に、どんな本か興味を持ってもらうためです。

□ display
　動 ～を表示する
□ advertising
　形 広告の
□ copy　名 宣伝文句

➡ 「帯」を英語で表現するなら belt です。

🙂 It plays an important role in book promotion.

本のPRにおいて重要な役割をになっています。

 How do you use a book *obi*?
本の帯の使い道は？

😊 There are people who leave it on, and people who throw it away as soon as they buy the book because it gets in the way of reading.

つけたままにする人や、読むのに邪魔なため、買ったらすぐに捨ててしまう人もいます。

😊 There are also people who collect book *obi*.

中には本の帯をコレクションしている人もいます。

🙂 Some people take it off and use it as a bookmark.

取ってしおりに使う人もいます。

 What kind of things are written on an *obi*?
帯にはどんなことが書かれているのですか？

😊 Information about the book that you can't get from the title is written.

タイトルだけじゃわからないような本についての情報が書かれます。

😊 A lot of them have praise for the book from famous people.

著名人の推薦コメントなどが書かれることも多いです。

😊 For things like reading promotions, the publisher might make all the *obi* match to stand out.

読書キャンペーンなどでは、出版社で統一した帯をかけて目立たせることもあります。

□ role 名 役；役割
□ promotion 名 販売促進

□ get in the way of ～の邪魔になる

□ collect 動 ～を集める

□ bookmark 名 しおり

□ praise 名 称賛

□ publisher 名 出版社
□ match 動 ～に一致する
□ stand out 目立つ

THEME 9 文具
Stationery

「消えるボールペン」の登場は、日本人の私たちにも驚きでしたが、その人気はもはや世界レベルのようですね！

英語で言うと？ --------------------------------

文具専門店：**stationery store**　おしゃれな：**fashionable (item)**　凝ったデザインの：**something with a fancy design**　色違いの：**of a different color**
品番：**product number**　サイズ違い：**different [wrong] size**

Photo: keisuke3 さんによる写真 AC からの写真

 ## What kind of stationery is popular with Japanese people?
日本人にはどんな文具が人気ですか？

Erasable ballpoint pens flew off the shelves when they were released, and are still a popular Japanese stationery item.

消えるボールペンは発売当初爆発的に売れ、今でも日本人の定番の文具として人気があります。

□ erasable
　形 消去可能な
□ fly off the shelves
　飛ぶように売れる

26

Masking tape that you can write on is popular among women, and it's used for wrapping presents, decorating photo albums, and sticking to foods in the freezer.

女性の間では字が書けるマスキングテープが人気で、プレゼントのラッピングに使ったり、アルバムのデコレーション、冷凍庫に入れる食品に貼ったりします。

Stickers are popular among girls, and you can collect them and exchange them with your friends. A sticker book for collecting stickers is also a popular item.

女の子にはシールが人気で、シールを集めたり、友達と交換して楽しみます。シールを貼るシール帳も人気のアイテムです。

Where can I buy stationery?
文具はどこで買えますか？

You can buy it at specialty stationery stores. There are large ones with many types.

専門の文房具店で買えます。たくさんの種類を揃えた大きな専門店があります。

Bookstores and convenience stores also sell stationery. There is a stationery corner in department stores.

本屋やコンビニでも文房具を扱っています。デパートなどでも文房具コーナーがあります。

There is "Bunbogu Cafe" in Shibuya where stationery is the theme. There, you can try over 5,000 types of stationery goods.

渋谷には「文房具カフェ」という、文房具をテーマにしたカフェがあります。そこでは5000種類以上の文房具が無料で試せます。

□ role　名 役；役割
□ promotion
　名 販売促進

□ specialty
　名 得意分野；特殊性

☞ 毎年新たな文具の新製品が世に出てきます。実用的で（practical）、画期的な（breakthrough）ものがたくさん！

THEME 10 招き猫
Manekineko

🔽 10

空前の猫ブームだからというわけではありませんが、縁起物の「招き猫」もいいお土産の一品です。東京の谷中には専門店もあります！

英語で言うと？

縁起もの：**lucky charm**　陶器：**ceramic**　商売繁盛：**thriving business**　小判：**oval**　縁結び：**marriage**　諸説あり：**existence of multiple theories**

Photo: yosomatu / PIXTA (ピクスタ)

What is that cat with its paw up?
手（前足）を挙げている猫はなんですか？

😊 It's a lucky charm called a *maneki-neko*.

招き猫と呼ばれる縁起物です。

😊 In the past, they were often made of ceramic, and you could buy them at places like shrines.

昔は陶器などで作られることが多く、神社などで買うことができました。

□ paw　**名** 足；手

□ lucky charm
　開運のお守り

□ ceramic
形 陶器の　**名** 陶磁器

28

Now they're made of lots of different materials like fabric and plastic, and you can buy them at places like souvenir stores.

現在は布やプラスチックなどいろんな素材で作られていて、土産屋などでも買えます。

□ material 名 素材

□ souvenir store 土産物屋

What do they mean?
どんな意味があるのですか？

Their paw faces down toward themselves, beckoning luck.

前足を自分に向けて、福を招いています。

□ paw 名 前足
□ beckon 動 ～に合図 [手招き] する

It's said that the right paw beckons money and will bring in business.

右足は、お金を招くと言われて商売繁盛をもたらすとされています。

It's said that the left paw beckons good fortune, and is good for luck and for conceiving a child.

左足は、縁を招くと言われて、縁結びや子授かりに良いとされています。

□ good fortune 幸運

Did they originate in Japan?
日本が発祥ですか？

It's said that they originated in Japan around the Edo period.

江戸時代ごろに日本で発祥したと言われています。

□ originate 動 由来する

There are various theories about their origin, but Imado Shrine in Asakusa and Gotokuji Temple in Setagaya are famous.

諸説ありますが、浅草の今戸神社や世田谷の豪徳寺が有名です。

□ various theories 諸説

There's also a theory that they originated at the Fushimi Inari Shrine in Kyoto.

京都の伏見稲荷大社が発祥だとする説もあります。

文化

THEME 11 都市伝説
Urban Legends

だれもが1つぐらいは耳にしたことがある「都市伝説」。ストーリーの背後にある日本の文化まで説明できたら大したものです！

井の頭公園にも伝説が…

英語で言うと？

友達の友達：**a friend of a friend**　噂話：**rumor**　口裂け女：**slit-mouthed woman**　人面犬：**human-faced dog**　真実味：**element of truth**
黄色いワーゲン：**yellow Volkswagen**

What's an urban legend?
都市伝説ってどんなもの？

It's rumors that everyone knows, usually told verbally from person to person.

人から人に基本的に口頭で広がった、誰もが知るような噂話のことです。

□ urban legend
都市伝説

□ rumor 名 うわさ
□ verbally
副 言語で

People say, "I heard from a friend of a friend," and tell the story like it really happened, but most of them never did.

「友達の友達から聞いた」などと、実際に起きたかのように語られますが、実際に起きていないことがほとんどです。

To add an element of truth, the person telling the story replaces things with local places. Most of the time, the origin of the story is unclear.

真実味が加わるように、身近な場所やものに置き換えられて語られます。（友達の友達など）発祥が不明なことがほとんどです。

□ add
　動 足す；加える
□ replace
　動 取り替える
□ unclear
　形 はっきりしない

What kinds of urban legends are there?
どんな都市伝説があるの？

"Kuchisake onna" is a woman in a long coat and a surgical mask. She takes off the mask and asks, "Am I beautiful?" but if you answer yes or no, you will be killed.

「口裂け女」はマスク姿にロングコートを着ています。マスクを外して「私って綺麗？」と尋ねてくるのですが、どう答えようと殺されてしまうと言われています。

□ surgical mask
　外科手術用マスク

There's also a deep-rooted legend about a "human-faced dog" that speaks human language and can run fast enough to overtake cars on the highway.

また人の顔を持った「人面犬」も根強く語られている都市伝説で、言葉を話す、高速道路では車を追い越すほど速く走れるという噂もあります。

□ deep-rooted
　根深い
□ overtake
　動 追い越す

It is said that if you hold up two mirrors so they reflect each other at midnight or 2 o'clock, your past and future will be reflected.

午前零時もしくは2時に合わせ鏡をすると、自分の過去と未来が映し出されると言われています。

□ reflect
　動 ～ (の像) を映す；
　反響する

THEME 12 妖怪
Youkai

『ゲゲゲの鬼太郎（Kitaro)』や浮世絵など、妖怪を扱った魅力的なコンテンツを紹介すると、視覚から一発で伝わりますね。

河鍋暁斎「妖怪と踊り猫」

英語で言うと？ -

怪談：**ghost story**　伝承民話：**folktale**　言い伝え：**legend**　架空の：**fictitious**
旅館：**inn**　怖い：**scary**　おとぼけ：**goofy**

What is a *youkai*?
妖怪って何？

It's a mysterious phenomenon or fictional creature based on Japanese folktales.

日本の伝承民話に基づく、不思議な現象や架空の生き物のことです。

- [ ] mysterious
  形 神秘的な
- [ ] phenomenon
  名 現象
- [ ] fictional
  形 架空の
- [ ] creature
  名 生き物
- [ ] folktale
  名 民間説話

It seems that when a phenomenon that people in the past couldn't understand occurred, it was considered the work of *youkai*.

昔の人たちが理解できない現象が起きた時にそれを妖怪の仕業だと考えたようです。

They exist all over Japan, and each area has its own legends.

日本各地に存在し、それぞれにいろんな言い伝えがあります。

□ exist 動 存在する
□ legend 名 伝説

What kind of *youkai* are in Japan?
日本にはどんな妖怪がいるの？

There are many, but the most famous are *kappa*, *tengu* and *oni*.

たくさん存在しますが、特に有名なのは河童や天狗、鬼などです。

The *kappa* is green and has a dish on its head. It's said to appear in rivers.

河童は緑色で頭にお皿がのっています。川に現れると言われています。

The *tengu* is red and has a very long nose. It has a fan made of leaves and flies around in the air.

天狗は赤く、鼻がとても高いのが特徴です。葉っぱのうちわを持っていて、空中を飛び回ります。

□ fan 名 扇
□ fly around
　　飛び回る

天狗は浮世絵にも多く登場する。こちらは鞍馬山の大天狗僧正坊のもとで、天狗を相手に武芸修行に励む牛若丸を描いた、河鍋暁斎の作品

33

Are you scared of *youkai*?

妖怪は怖いの？

There are scary *youkai*, but there are also funny and kind *youkai*.

怖い妖怪もいますが、ユーモラスだったり、優しい妖怪もいます。

The *zashikiwarashi* appears in old *ryokan*, and people who see it are said to advance in their careers.

座敷わらしは古い旅館などに現れ、見た人は出世すると言われています。

It is said that if you meet an *azukiarai youkai*, which laughs as it grinds *azuki* beans, you will get married soon.

笑いながらあずきをといでいる、あずき洗いという妖怪に出会うと、早くお嫁に行けると言われています。

□ scare
動 (人を)怖がらせる

□ scary 形 恐ろしい

□ advance 動 進歩する；昇進する

□ career
名 職業；経歴

□ grind
〜をひく；こすり合わせる

歌川広景による『江戸名所道戯盡二 両国の夕立』、歌川広重の名所江戸百景『大はしあたけの夕立』を題材とした滑稽画。誤って川に落ちた雷神から尻子玉を奪おうと河童が襲い掛かるが、雷神も屁で応戦する情景を描いている。

おばけ
Ghosts

 13

海外にも幽霊話はあると思いますが、ここはひとつ Japanese Style の "由緒正しい" お化けを英語でご案内しましょう。

月岡芳年 (左)「新形三十六怪撰　皿やしきに於菊の霊」(右)「月百姿　源氏夕顔巻」

英語で言うと？

先祖の霊：**spirit of our ancestors**　三途の川：**acheron (river of woe)**
極楽：**paradise**　地獄：**hell**　廃墟：**ruins**　心霊スポット：**haunted place**

(左) Photo: Licensed under Public Domain via Wikimedia Commons / Flickr / (右) Photo: 国立国会図書館ウェブサイト

Do Japanese people believe in ghosts?
日本人はおばけを信じていますか？

😊 Some people do, some people don't.

信じている人と信じていない人がいます。

😊 It's said that the spirits of our ancestors return home during *Obon* in summer, so ghosts often appear during that time.

夏のお盆は先祖の霊が帰ってくると言われていて、おばけが出やすいと言われています。

□ spirit
　名 (死者の) 魂
□ ancestor　名 先祖

35

◉ Because of that, in summer people make haunted houses and there are special programs on television.

そのため、夏はお化け屋敷ができたり、テレビなどでも特集が組まれることがあります。

□ haunted house
幽霊屋敷

 ## Where do ghosts appear?
どんな場所に出るのですか？

◉ People say they appear in graveyards and abandoned places like hospitals.

墓場や病院などの廃墟などに出ると言われています。

□ graveyard
名 墓地

💬 こわい話をしているとよく登場する「金縛り」という現象は、英語でsleep paralysis と言います。

◉ Some people say that there are ghosts that appear in the toilet at night, and so there are children who are scared to go to the toilet at night.

夜トイレに出るおばけもいると言われているので、夜のトイレを怖がる子供もいます。

◉ Tunnels in the mountains are also said to be ghost spots.

山の中のトンネルもおばけスポットとされています。

 ## What are some famous ghosts?
どんなおばけが有名ですか？

◉ People often imagine Japanese ghosts as having no feet, wearing white *kimono*, and being women with long hair. The image of ghosts painted by old painters has permeated Japanese culture.

日本のおばけは足がないことが多く、白い着物を着ていて、髪が長い女性のイメージです。昔の画家が描いた幽霊のイメージがそのまま浸透しています。

□ imagine
動 想像する
□ image
名 像；イメージ
□ permeate 動 ～
に広がる

● In the past, Okiku, who appears at wells, was famous, and even now her story is performed on stage, and exorcisms are conducted.

昔は、井戸に出ると言われたお菊さんが有名で、今でも舞台などでその怪談を上演する際はお祓いなどを行います。

● The ghost of Hanako, who appears in toilets, is famous as a school ghost.

学校にでるおばけとしては、トイレの花子さんが有名です。

☐ well 名 井戸
☐ perform 動 上演する
☐ exorcism 名 悪魔祓い
☐ conduct 動 導く；行う

田んぼや墓地や土手で目にすることが多い彼岸花。名前の由来は、「秋のお彼岸ごろに開花するから」や「毒を有するので食べたら死ぬ＝彼岸に行くしかないから」など複数の説がある。見る人をひきつける独特な形状をもつこの花は、英語では red spider lily や red magic lily と表現される。日本語でも、曼珠沙華をはじめ、死人花 (しびとばな)、地獄花 (じごくばな)、幽霊花 (ゆうれいばな) ほか、別名がたくさんある (ちなみに曼珠沙華はサンスクリット語のマンジュシャカ (赤い) からきているが、そのもともとの意味は「伝説上の天界の花」)。
晩夏から秋にかけての季節が見ごろで、写真の巾着田 (埼玉県日高市) がつとに有名。その規模は500万本ともいわれている。

不思議なマナー
Strange Manners

THEME 14

 14

普段当たり前に実践している「マナー」の一部では、外国人の目には不思議に映るものも少なくないようです！ 簡単な英語で説明してみましょう！

「つまらないもの」にはこんな理由があったのです！

英語で言うと？

(電話を)切る：**hang up**　失礼な：**rude**　礼儀正しい：**polite**　目上の人：**higher-ranking person**　手土産：**hospitality gift**　粗品：**small gift**

Photo: くまちゃん / PIXTA (ピクスタ)

Why don't you hang up the phone?
電話を先に切らないのはなぜ？

It's because people think that the one who hangs up first is trying to end the conversation quickly, and it's rude to the other person.

先に切るのは、「話を早く切り上げようとしている」と思われ、相手に失礼とされているからです。

☐ hang up the phone　電話を切る

☐ conversation 名 会話

☐ quickly 副 素早く

☐ rude 形 無礼な

38

Generally, it's thought to be polite if the person who called hangs up first.

基本的にはかけたほうが先に切るのがマナーとされています。

□ polite
形 礼儀正しい

If the other person is someone above you or a customer, you wait until they hang up.

相手が目上の人やお客様であれば、相手が切るまで待ちます。

Why do you say, "It's boring," when you give a present?

プレゼントを渡すときにどうして「つまらないもの」と言うの？

In Japan, there is a custom of returning gifts that are given to you, so we say that so that the person doesn't feel the need to worry.

日本人は贈り物をされたら返す習慣があるので、その気遣いをさせないためだと言われています。

□ boring
形 退屈な；つまらない

We say that to express that it's not a big thing, and we're not expecting anything in return.

わざわざお礼を返してもらうような、大したものではありませんよ、という意味を込めて使います。

□ express 動 述べる
□ expect
動 予期する
□ in return
返礼として

It's not that we actually give boring gifts.

本当につまらないものをあげているわけではありません。

Why do you stand to one side on the escalator in places like train stations?

どうして駅などのエスカレーターではじに寄るの？

We leave one side open for people who are in a hurry.

急いでいる人のために片側を空けます。

○ 関東では右側を空け、関西では左側を空けます。なお、このトピックは、P150 で詳しく解説します！

However, it's actually dangerous to walk on escalators, so it's banned.

ただ、本来そこを歩くことは危険なため、禁止されています。

□ ban 動 ～を禁じる

迷信
Superstitions

15

最近ではあまり信じない＆気にしない人も多いかもしれませんが、話のネタとしては異文化交流的側面からも、面白いのではないでしょうか。

茶柱！

英語で言うと？ -

霊柩車：**hearse**　救急車：**ambulance**　死者：**deceased person**　風水：**feng shui**　恵方巻：**thick sushi roll eaten for luck**　初物：**first of the season**

Are there superstitions in Japan?
日本に迷信は存在しますか？

There are lots of superstitions about good and bad luck.

縁起のいい迷信や悪い迷信などたくさん存在します。

☐ superstition
名 迷信

There are also superstitions about things in daily life such as food.

その他、食事にまつわるものなど生活の中にも迷信があります。

☐ daily life
日常生活

😊 Young people don't believe in superstition as much as people in the past did.

昔の人ほど迷信を信じ、若い子は気にしない子も多いです。

What are some superstitions about good and bad luck?

縁起の悪い迷信、良い迷信は？

😊 People say that if a hearse or ambulance passes and you don't hide your thumb, you won't be there to see the death of your parents.

霊柩車や救急車が通ったら親指を隠さないと親の死に目に会えないとされています。

☐ hearse 名 霊柩車
☐ ambulance
　名 救急車

😊 It's said that having one of your tea leaves stand on its edge is good luck. A four-leaf clover is also a lucky item.

茶柱が立つといいことがあると言われています。四つ葉のクローバーも幸運のアイテムです。

☐ edge 名 端
➡ 茶柱については、P178 で詳しく説明しています。

What does "north pillow" mean?

北枕ってなんですか？

😊 It means sleeping with your pillow facing north.

北に枕を向けて寝ることです。

😊 The dead are laid down with their pillow facing north, so it's said that sleeping that way is unlucky.

死者を北枕で寝かせるため、縁起がよくないとされています。

☐ dead 名 死者
☐ laid down
　〜を横たえる

😊 But, in feng shui, there is the idea that a north-facing pillow is good, and recently there are an increasing number of people who don't care.

ただ風水では、北枕が良いというする説もあり、最近では気にしない人も増えています。

☐ feng shui 風水
☐ increasing
　形 増加する

文化

○○女子、○○男子
___ Joshi, ___ Danshi

「○○女子」「○○男子」という概念も、日本独特のカルチャーを端的に表します。ただし移り変わりが早いので、最新の情報を常にチェック！

英語で言うと？ -

性格：**personality**　ボーイズラブ：**comic or novel about male homosexuality**
理系：**science**　文系：**humanities**　体育会系：**physical education**
文化系：**culture**

Photo: bee / PIXTA (ピクスタ)

What does "___ joshi" mean?
○○女子ってどういう意味？

😊 "___ joshi" means a woman who has a hobby and really loves it.

○○には趣味などが入り、それをこよなく愛する女性を指します。

The word "joshi" was originally used for younger women, but now it is used for women of all ages.

通常「女子」とは低年齢層に対して使われていましたが、今では年齢を問わず、女性全般に対して使われます。

It's usually used in things that are regarded as male hobbies. On the other hand, a man who likes feminine hobbies is called a "__ danshi".

☐ regarded as
　～とみなされる
☐ feminine 形 女の

たいてい、世間では男性の趣味とされるものであることが多いです。反対に、女性が好むであろうものを好きな男性を「〇〇男子」と呼んだりします。

What kinds of "__ joshi" are there?
どんな種類がありますか?

Women who actively approach men are called "carnivorous girls".

☐ actively
　副 活発に
☐ approach
　動 ～に近づく
☐ carnivorous
　形 肉食の

男性に積極的にアプローチする女性は、「肉食系女子」と呼ばれます。

There are also many sports-related types such as "pu joshi" who love professional wrestling, "sumo joshi" who are sumo fans, and "carp joshi" who are female fans of the Hiroshima Carp baseball team.

☐ sports-related
　スポーツに関する
☐ professional
　wrestling
　プロレスリング

また、プロレス好きの「プ女子」、相撲ファンの「相撲女子(スー女)」、広島カープという野球チームの女性ファン「カープ女子」など、スポーツに関連するものが多く存在します。

Also, people who look good with glasses are called "megane danshi" and "megane joshi".

また、メガネが似合っていて魅力的な人を、「メガネ男子」、「メガネ女子」などと呼びます。

What kinds of "__ danshi" are there?

○○男子にはどんなのがありますか？

● Types of men that can get along with women, like "sweets danshi" who like sweets, and "creamy-type danshi" who are gentle, kind, and handsome, are popular.

スイーツが好きな「スイーツ男子」や穏やかで優しく見た目も美しい「クリーミー系男子」など、女性とも仲良くできるタイプの男性が人気です。

● Men who are passive in romantic relationships are called "herbivorous danshi", and those who are not interested at all are called "fasting danshi".

恋愛に消極的な男性は「草食系男子」と呼ばれ、まったく興味がない人を「絶食系男子」と呼びます。

● Also, men who work with their bodies and are muscular are called "gatenkei danshi" and "gatenkei".

また、体を使った仕事に就いていて、ガタイのいい男子は「ガテン系男子」や「ガテン系」と呼ばれます。

□ get along with
（人と）仲良くする

□ passive
形 受動的な
□ romantic relationship
恋愛関係
□ herbivorous
形 草食性の
□ fasting 名 断食

□ muscular
形 筋肉の発達した

44

THEME 17

ハロウィン
Halloween

⬇17

近年急激に大イベント化しているハロウィンですが、特に欧米からのお客様に対しては、日本風の楽しみ方について、説明の必要があるでしょう。

2017年ハロウィン当日の渋谷駅前スクランブル交差点

英語で言うと？ -

限定商品：**limited-edition product**　社会問題：**social issue**　出動：**deploy**　アニメキャラ：**anime character**　話題の：**talked-about**　有名人：**celebrity**

Photo: momo / PIXTA (ピクスタ)

What's halloween like in Japan?
日本のハロウィンはどんな雰囲気ですか？

😀 In recent years, its become one of the biggest annual events along with Christmas and Valentine's Day.

ここ数年、クリスマスやバレンタインと並び、1年の中でも大きな盛り上がりを見せるイベントとなりました。

☐ annual
形 年に一度の；毎年恒例の

🎃 Halloween products start to fill stores in September, and in October city displays also change to Halloween colors.

9月の初めにはグッズが店頭に並び始め、10月になると街のディスプレイもハロウィン一色になります。

🎃 In Halloween season, restaurants also have limited edition products like pumpkin flavor.

飲食店でもハロウィンシーズンには、パンプキン味などの限定商品を提供します。

□ edition
名 (刊行物の) 版

What do Japanese people do on Halloween?
日本人はハロウィンに何をするのですか？

🎃 Halloween events are held in big cities, and parades are also held.

大きな都市ではハロウィンイベントなどが開催され、パレードなどが行われます。

🎃 Children do dress up in costumes and go around neighborhoods to get candy, but they mostly do it at events, and don't knock on doors like in America.

子供も仮装をして近所を回りお菓子をもらいますが、イベントなどの中で行うことがほとんどで、アメリカのように近所を突然訪ねることはありません。

🎃 Adults have fun doing cosplay and walk around the city, or go drinking.

大人はコスプレを楽しみ、街を練り歩いたり、飲み会をしたりします。

➐ 渋谷のスクランブル交差点 (scramble intersection) は毎年ものすごい混雑が見られます。

□ have fun 楽しむ
□ cosplay
動 (〜の) コスプレをする 名 コスプレ
➐ cosplay は costume play とも言えます。

What kinds of costumes do people wear?
どんなコスプレをするのですか？

🎃 People don't dress up in scary costumes as much as in America, and anime characters are more popular with both men and women.

アメリカほど、怖い格好をする人は多くなく、アニメのキャラクターなどの方が男女共に人気があります。

🎃 Families and groups of friends do group costumes with characters from the same anime.

家族や友達でお揃いのコスチュームにしたり、同じアニメの登場キャラクターで揃えたりします。

🎃 There are also people who dress up as celebrities that were popular in Japan that year.

その年日本で話題になった有名人や、流行った芸人などの格好をする人も多いです。

☐ celebrity
名 有名人；名声

近年の日本では45ページの写真のような感じで大人たちの間でも盛り上がっているハロウィン。そしてアメリカのハロウィンといえばこの写真のような感じで、仮装した子供たちが練り歩き、Trick or treat! と、お菓子をねだるイメージですが、ハロウィンの起源はアメリカではありません。

そのルーツは、遠い昔の北ヨーロッパでケルト文化を築いた人々の伝統行事にあり、この日（10月31日）は先祖の霊が家に帰ってくる日、死者たちの霊を供養する日とされていたそうです。ちょっと日本の「お盆」みたいですね。

その後、中世キリスト教の影響でハロウィンという名前になっていったわけですが、死者の霊を供養する慣習を忘れないために、死者を模した仮装をして＝死者の霊になりきって、家々を回るという内容が盛り込まれていったそうです。

そして19世紀前半にたくさんのアイルランド人がアメリカに渡ってからは、もともとはカブで作られていたランタンがカボチャになり、死者の霊を供養する慣習に関しては、「お菓子をくれなきゃ（ご先祖様を供養しないと）いたずらするぞ」と言って子供たちが家々を訪ねるイベントに変化したということです。

Photo: iStockphoto.com / Rawpixel

47

メイドカフェ
Maid Cafes

 18

メイドカフェといえば「萌え」がフィーチャーされがちですが、そうではないタイプのカフェもあるので、ご案内の際には確認しましょう。

英語で言うと？ ---

チャージ料がかかる：**a fee is charged**　追加料金：**additional charge**　写真撮影：**photo shoot**　老舗：**long-standing store**　ご主人様：**master**　執事：**butler**

Photo: Fast&Slow / PIXTA (ピクスタ)

When did "meido kafe", or maid cafes, first appear in Japan?

日本でメイドカフェができたのはいつ？

It is said that they began at coffee shops in Ginza from the end of the Meiji period into the Taisho period.

明治時代末期から大正時代の銀座にあった喫茶店が始まりと言われています。

At the time, it appears that cute, kimono-clad waitresses were serving customers.

□ kimono-clad
着物姿の

当時は、着物姿のかわいいウエイトレスが接客していたようです。

At a long-established maid cafe that opened in Akihabara in 2001, waitresses wearing long maid outfits served customers just as they would at a traditional coffee shop.

□ long-established
長い歴史を持つ
□ outfit
名 (一揃いの) 衣服
□ traditional
形 伝統的な

2001年秋葉原でオープンした老舗のメイドカフェは、丈が長めのメイド服を着たウエイトレスが普通の喫茶店のように接客します。

Do services differ from one maid cafe to another?

メイドカフェそれぞれでサービスが違うの？

There are two types — one where customers are served as they would be at a traditional cafe, and one where waitresses communicate more with customers.

□ differ from
〜とは異なる

□ communicate
動 交信する

普通の喫茶店のように接客をするカフェと、お客さんとたくさんコミュニケーションをとるカフェの2種類があります。

There are cafes where waitresses draw pictures with ketchup on orders of omelette rice, and even feed customers.

□ feed
動 〜に食物を与える

お客さんが注文したオムライスにケチャップで絵を描いたり、お客さんの口に料理を運んでくれるカフェなどもあります。

There are also cafes where they take pictures and play games with customers, or dance on stage.

お客さんと一緒に写真撮影をしたりゲームをするカフェや、メイドがステージでダンスなどをするカフェもあります。

THEME 19 コスプレ
Cosplay

🔽 19

コミケやゲームショウなどはもちろんのこと、マラソン大会やコンサートなどでコスプレしている人を目にすることが多くなりましたね。

「サブカルの聖地」中野ブロードウェイ

英語で言うと？ -

同人誌：**fanzine** 同人サークル：**fan club** 歩行者天国：**pedestrian's paradise**
コスプレイヤー：**costume player** 装身具：**accessories** カラコン：**colored
contact lens**

写真提供：(公財) 東京観光財団

What's cosplay?
コスプレって何？

It's short for costume play, and it means wearing the costume of a character from an anime or other work.

コスチュームプレイの略で、アニメなどのキャラクターのコスチュームで扮装することです。

☐ be short for
　〜の省略である
☐ costume play
　コスプレ

It's not just anime, people dress up and wear make-up to look like video game characters and fashion-focused band members.

アニメだけではなく、ゲームのキャラクターのファンやビジュアルバンドのファンも、キャラやメンバーと同じような格好やメイクをします。

People who cosplay are called cosplayers or "reiya", and some of them have many fans of their own.

コスプレをする人はコスプレイヤーもしくはレイヤーと呼ばれ、中にはたくさんのファンがいるカリスマ的存在もいます。

Where do people cosplay?
どんなところでコスプレするのですか？

At Comiket, which is the world's largest self-published comics convention, anime fans attend in character costumes.

コミケと呼ばれる世界最大の同人誌即売会で、アニメのファンがキャラクターに扮して参加するようになりました。

There are also people who cosplay at fashion-focused band concerts and music festivals.

ビジュアルバンドのコンサートや、音楽フェスなどでもコスプレする人がいます。

An increasing number of runners run at marathons and other events in cosplay.

フルマラソンなどの大会でもコスプレをしながら走るランナーが増えています。

□ wear make-up
化粧をする

□ self-published
形 自費出版の
□ convention
名 大会；総会
□ attend
動 ～に出席 [参加] する

🔵 「コミケ」の正式名称はコミックマーケット (Comic Market) で、年に 2 回開催されている

文化

Where do people get their costumes?
衣装はどこで手に入れる？

You can buy them at cosplay speciality sites, or for famous characters, at mass retailers in cities.

コスプレ専門のサイトなどで手に入れたり、街の量販店でも有名なキャラクターであれば購入できます。

☐ speciality
名 得意分野；専門技能

☐ mass retailer
量販店

They're also sold at anime merchandise stores, but there aren't many sizes or varieties.

アニメグッズ専門店などでも販売していますが、サイズや種類はそれほど豊富ではないでしょう。

There are also a lot of people who make their own costumes.

自分で衣装を手作りしている人も多くいます。

Popular cosplayers often spend a lot of time and effort making their own costumes.

カリスマ的存在の人たちの多くは手間暇かけて自作しています。

☐ effort 名 努力

Photo: piyato / PIXTA / PIXTA（ピクスタ）

THEME 20

イルミネーション
Illumination

↓ 20

文化

都会の街中を飾り付けるものからテーマパークが大々的に行うものまで、特に冬はさまざまなイルミネーションが楽しめます。寒さ対策を万全に！

東京・丸の内のイルミネーション

英語で言うと？ -

寒さ対策：**cold-weather measures**　カイロ：**disposable heat pack**　耳あて：**earmuffs**　人気スポット：**popular spot**：　恒例の：**customary**　消費電力：**electricity consumption**

写真提供：(公財) 東京観光財団

Does illumination have a long history in Japan?

日本にイルミネーションは昔からあるのですか？

It's said that the beginning of illumination in Japan was the ship viewing type during the Meiji Era when ships in Kobe Port shone their lights on the surface of the water.

☐ shine　動 光らせる
☐ surface　名 表面

53

明治時代、神戸沖において行われた観艦式で、艦船が発光して海面を照らしたことが日本のイルミネーションの始まりだと言われています。

 Around the same time, the entrances of expos held in cities such as Osaka were decorated with electric lights, and it seems it had a big impact on the people who saw it for the first time.

同じ頃、大阪などの都市で開かれた博覧会の入り口を電飾で飾り付け、初めて見る人々に大きな衝撃を与えたようです。

□ expo 名 博覧会 (= exposition)
□ electric light 電灯
□ impact 名 影響 (力)；衝撃

It seems that import stores in Ginza decorated with Christmas lights every year and were a hot topic.

銀座にあった輸入品を扱う店が毎年クリスマスシーズンに飾り付けを行い、話題を呼んでいたようです。

□ import 名 輸入 (すること)

What kinds of illumination are there?
どんな種類のイルミネーションがあるのですか？

Trees on the street are decorated with single or multi-color lights. Currently, illumination using LED lights is mainstream.

街路樹を単色、もしくはカラフルに電飾で飾り付けます。今はLEDを使ったものが主流です。

□ multi-color 多色の；色とりどりの
□ currently 副 一般に；今のところ
□ mainstream 名 本流

The projection of images onto buildings, which is called projection mapping, is also popular.

プロジェクションマッピングというプロジェクターを使って建物などに映像を投影する演出も人気があります。

□ projection 名 投射；映像
□ projection mapping プロジェクションマッピング

Amusement parks and city buildings also have fancy performances in the courtyards, by setting up light decorations on lawns and holding light shows at specific times.

芝生など電飾を敷き詰めて、時間によって光のショーが行われるなど、遊園地や都内のビルの敷地内などは派手な演出をします。

□ fancy 形 しゃれた；派手な
□ courtyard 名 中庭
□ lawn 名 芝生

Where can I see it?

どこで見ることができますか？

● During the Christmas season, the entire city is illuminated. If you live in a big city, you can usually see it.

クリスマスシーズンは街全体でイルミネーションをしています。大きな都市であれば大抵見ることができます。

● Amusement parks and theme parks also offer beautiful illuminations at night.

遊園地やテーマパークなども夜は綺麗なイルミネーションを見ることができます。

● Christmas decorations permeate even in ordinary households, and there are some families that lively decorate.

一般家庭でもクリスマスの飾り付けは浸透していて、賑やかに飾り付けている家庭もあります。

□ entire 形 全体の

□ offer
動 申し出る；提供する

□ permeate
動 ～に広がる
□ ordinary
形 いつもの；当たり前の
□ household
名 家族；家庭
□ lively
形 元気いっぱいの；陽気な

文化

こちらもおなじみ、東京の原宿・表参道のクリスマスイルミネーション

写真提供：(公財) 東京観光財団

ラブホ
Love Hotels

🔽 21

訪日観光客の宿泊先として意外にも人気な「ラブホ」。その特徴やビジネスホテルやシティホテルとの違いを英語で表現してみましょう。

渋谷のラブホテル街（2014年）

英語で言うと？ -

回転ベッド：**revolving bed**　鏡張り：**mirrored**　プライバシー保護：**privacy protection**　繁華街：**busy downtown street**　未成年：**minor**　入店禁止：**entry prohibited**

Photo: Licensed under Public Domain via Wikimedia Commons / Flickr　帰属：Joe Mabel

What are love hotels?
ラブホテルって何ですか？

😀 They're basically hotels where couples go to have sex.

基本的にはカップルが性交渉を行うことを目的としたホテルです。

☐ have sex
性交渉をもつ

● Most of them only offer rooms and there are no restaurants or other facilities.

素泊まりであることがほとんどでレストランなどの他の施設は併設されていません。

● But in recent years, there are love hotels that come with open-air baths and all-you-can-eat sweets.

☐ all-you-can-eat
食べ放題の

ただ近年では、露天風呂を併設したり、スイーツの食べ放題ができるラブホテルもあります。

● The price to stay there is comparatively cheap compared to regular hotels.

☐ compare
動 ～と比べる

通常のホテルよりは比較的宿泊費は安く設定されています。

What's the difference to a regular hotel?
普通のホテルとの違いは？

● As well as staying overnight like at a regular hotel, you can stay for a period of time called a "rest".

☐ overnight
副 一晩
形 一泊用の
名 一泊旅行
☐ a period of time
期間

普通のホテルにある宿泊の他に、休憩コースという時間で区切った滞在の仕方もあります。

● Most have a panel to choose a room at the front desk, and you choose by pushing a button.

☐ panel 名 パネル

フロントには大抵部屋を選ぶパネルがあり、ボタンを押して選択します。

● The entrance is often concealed with trees and walls so people can't see it.

☐ conceal 動 隠す

入口が人目につきにくいように、木や壁といった目隠しのようなものが置かれていることが多いです。

ラブホテルと普通のホテルとの最大の違いは、サービスとして避妊具 (condom) が部屋に置かれていること。かつては自動精算 (automatic settlement) システムも特徴でしたが、最近ではビジネスホテルなどでも自動になっているところがありますね！

マスク
Surgical Masks

インフルエンザや花粉症に悩まされる冬から春の季節、特に都心部の通勤時間帯の光景は、欧米などからの観光客にはぎょっとされることも。

英語で言うと？ --

予防：**prevention**　流行している：**going around**　不織布：**non-woven fabric**
プリーツ：**pleats**　使い捨て：**disposable**　機能的なマスク：**functional mask**

Photo: photoB さんによる写真 AC からの写真

Why do so many Japanese people wear surgical masks?

どうして日本人の多くはよくマスクをするのですか？

They wear them so that colds and other illnesses that are going around aren't spread through crowds.

□ illness　名 病気

流行している風邪などに人混みの中で感染しないように装着します。

58

◉ We wear them when we have a cold as a courtesy so we don't give our cold to other people.

自分が風邪を引いているときにくしゃみなどで他人にうつさないようエチケットとしてつけます。

☐ as a courtesy
礼儀として

◉ People with hayfever wear them in pollen season to prevent it.

花粉シーズンは花粉症の人はマスクをつけて防御します。

 ## What kinds of masks are there?
どんなマスクがありますか？

◉ Generally they have pleats so you can spread them to cover your face.

通常はプリーツ状になっていて、広げて自分の顔のサイズに合わせます。

☐ pleat
名 ひだ；プリーツ

◉ Black masks are popular with men.

男性には黒いマスクも人気があります。

◉ There are also types of masks that are designed to stay on, or to not fog up your glasses.

メイクの落ちにくいもの、メガネの曇らないものなどもあります。

☐ stay on
（居）続ける
☐ fog
動 〜を曇らせる

Photo: iStockphoto.com / gyro

文
化

59

THEME 23 銭湯
Sento

 23

銭湯も外国人にしてみれば立派な「日本体験」。入店から退店までの基本ルールや設備などについても、英語で言えるようにしておきましょう。

富士山の壁画はお約束!

英語で言うと?

番台：**attendant's booth**　下駄箱：**shoe box**　脱衣所：**dressing room**　男湯：**men's bath**　女湯：**women's bath**　コーヒー牛乳：**coffee-flavored milk**

Photo: おがさわらさんによる写真ACからの写真

Is a *sento* different to an *onsen*?
銭湯って温泉と違うの?

An *onsen* is where hot water comes out of the ground naturally, and a *sento* is a man-made bathing area.

温泉が自然から湧き出るお湯であるのに対して、銭湯は人工的に作られた浴場です。

Sento means that you can borrow hot water for money.

☐ man-made
形 人工の
☐ bathing area
水浴場

☐ borrow　動 借りる

60

銭湯は、「お金を払って湯を借りる」という意味です。

 It's said that it began when Buddhists provided baths to the common people as part of their missionary activities.

仏教の布教活動の一環で、庶民に風呂を提供したのが始まりだと言われています。

- □ common people
  一般人；庶民
- □ as part of
  〜の一部として
- □ missionary
  activity　布教活動

 What kind of place is a super *sento*?
スーパー銭湯ってどんなところ？

 It's a *sento* that's more large scale than usual.

一般的な銭湯よりも大規模な銭湯です。

- □ large scale
  大規模

 They have facilities like saunas, massages and jacuzzis.

サウナやマッサージ、ジャグジーなどの施設が充実しています。

- □ sauna　名 サウナ
- □ jacuzzi　名 泡風呂

 Some also have food and *karaoke*.

食事処やカラオケなどが併設されているところもあります。

 What is the etiquette at *sentos*?
銭湯のマナーは？

 In the changing room, fold up your clothing and put it in a basket.

脱衣所で衣類は畳んでカゴに入れましょう。

- □ etiquette
  名 エチケット
- □ changing room
  更衣室
- □ fold up　畳む

 When you enter the bathroom, wash yourself lightly in the shower.

浴室に入ったら、シャワーで軽く体の汚れを落とします。

- □ bathroom
  名 浴室
- □ lightly　副 軽く

 Don't put your towel in the bathtub.

タオルは湯船につけないようにしましょう。

風呂の洗い場
Washing Areas

🔽 24

銭湯だけでなくホテルの個室やホームステイ先でも、日本式のお風呂での
洗い場の使い方や入浴のルール説明が必要になることは多いです。

公衆浴場の洗い場

英語で言うと？ -

洗い場：**washing area**　蛇口：**faucet**　洗面器：**sink**　ペンキ絵：**painting**
タイル絵：**tile picture**　湯船：**bathtub**

Photo: charly / PIXTA (ピクスタ)

What kinds of places have washing areas outside the bath?

お風呂の洗い場があるところはどんなところですか？

🗨 The bathroom in a typical home is usually divided into a bathtub and a washing area.

一般的な家庭の家のお風呂は大抵浴槽と洗い場に分かれています。

🗨 Public baths such as hotels, inns, and hot springs usually have separate washing areas.

ホテルや旅館、温泉等の公衆浴場も通常洗い場が別にあります。

- ☐ bath 名 風呂場
- ☐ typical 形 典型的な
- ☐ public bath 公衆浴場
- ☐ inn 名 宿屋
- ☐ separate 形 離れた

62

🚿 There are many unit bathrooms where space is limited, such as single person apartments and business hotels.

一人暮らし用の部屋やビジネスホテルなど広さが限られたところはユニットバスが多いです。

How do I use a washing area?
洗い場の使い方は？

🚿 It's a place with showers and faucets, mainly for washing your body.

シャワーと蛇口がついていて、主に体を洗うための場所です。

☐ faucet　名 蛇口

🚿 You use the chair and basin in the washing area, and wash your face and hair there too.

洗い場に置いてある椅子や洗面器を使って、顔や髪の毛もそこで洗います。

☐ basin
　名 たらい；洗面器

🚿 I use the shower in the washing area to clean the bathroom.

洗い場のシャワーを使って浴室を掃除したりします。

Is there etiquette for the washing area in public facilities?
公共施設の洗い場でのマナーはありますか？

🚿 Avoid splashing other people when taking a shower.

シャワーをかける時、他の人に水しぶきがかからないようにしましょう。

☐ avoid
　動 ～するのを防ぐ
☐ splash
　動 (しぶきで) ～を濡らす

🚿 After you use it, you should wash away soap and dirt with the shower water.

使用後は簡単にシャワーの水で泡などの汚れを流しましょう。

☐ wash away
　洗い流す
☐ dirt　名 汚れ

🚿 Return the chairs and basins you used to where they were originally.

使った椅子や湯桶などはもともとあった場所に戻しましょう。

☐ originally
　副 もともと

THEME 25 スーパー銭湯
Super *Sento*

📥 25

お風呂だけでなく食事や仮眠設備など多様なサービスが提供されるスーパー銭湯や健康ランドも、気軽に日本独特の文化が体験できるスポット。

スーパー銭湯極楽湯名取店（2014年撮影）

英語で言うと？ --------------------------------------

サウナ：**sauna**　水風呂：**cold bath**　電気風呂：**electric bath**　ジェット風呂：**whirlpool bath**　天然温泉：**natural hot spring**　岩盤浴：**bedrock bath**

What kind of place is a super *sento*?
スーパー銭湯ってどんなところですか？

😊 It is a particularly large-scale paid public bath.

お金を払って入る公共のお風呂の中でも、規模が大きい施設のことです。

😊 They also have substantial facilities besides baths, such as restaurants.

食事処など銭湯以外の施設も充実しています。

☐ large-scale
　大型の；大規模の

☐ substantial
　形 頑丈な；相当な；十分な

😊 And they have further evolved into super public baths known as "Health Land."

スーパー銭湯がさらに進化し大規模になったものが「健康ランド」です。

 ## What features do they have?
どんな特徴があるんですか？

😊 You can enjoy various types of baths such as whirlpool baths, *utaseyu*, and open-air baths.

ジェットバス、打たせ湯、露天風呂など様々な種類のお風呂が楽しめます。

☐ whirlpool bath
泡風呂
☐ open-air
屋外の；露天の

😊 There are places where you can take a break after bathing, such as cafes, massages, and hairdressers.

湯上りに休憩できる場所や、カフェ、マッサージ、理髪店などがあります。

☐ hairdressers
名 美容師；美容院

😊 Many facilities offer souvenirs, and some people buy souvenirs for their families and friends.

お土産などが充実している施設もあり、家族や友人などにお土産を買って帰る人もいます。

 ## What kind of system is it?
どんなシステム？

😊 First take off your shoes and put them in a locker.

まず靴を脱いでロッカーに入れます。

😊 When you pay, you will be given a wristband with a locker key for the changing room.

料金を支払うと更衣室ロッカーのリストバンドが渡されます。

☐ wristband
名 リストバンド
☐ changing room
更衣室

🐵 You keep the wristband on your wrist the whole time, until you get out of the bath.

リストバンドは湯上りまでずっと手首につけておきましょう。

🐵 Depending on the facility, some might record your use of the facility on the wristband, and bill you at the end.

施設によっては、そのリストバンドに館内の利用履歴が記録され、最後に清算となるところもあります。

□ bill
🔲 請求書を送る

🐵 Towels are not usually given, so you need to rent or purchase them if necessary.

タオルなどは通常ついて来ないので、必要な場合は有料で借りたり、購入したりする必要があります。

□ rent
🔲 賃借［賃貸］する

東京のお台場にて2003年にオープンした「大江戸温泉物語」は、日本初となる"温泉テーマパーク"。単なる"お風呂"ではなく、館内には江戸の縁日が展開されており、懐かしい日本ならではのアトラクションが目いっぱい楽しめる。ほかにもゲームコーナーや占いもあり、老若男女だれでも楽しい時間を過ごすことができる。
ちなみに今では全国36ヵ所に『温泉旅館・ホテル・日帰り温浴施設・テーマパーク』が展開されており、それぞれの施設が独自の雰囲気をもっているので、旅先で見かけたら立ち寄ってみるのも面白いかも！

66

THEME 26 旅館
Ryokan

純日本的な宿泊体験ができる旅館に関心をもつ訪日観光客も多いです。楽しみ方やお部屋についての基本情報をご案内してみましょう！

英語で言うと？ --

宿：**inn**　木造建築：**wooden structure**　露天風呂：**open-air bath**　荷を下ろす：**organize one's luggage**　雰囲気：**atmosphere**　ご当地の銘菓：**local snack**

Photo: aoi / PIXTA（ピクスタ）

Is a *ryokan* different from a hotel?
旅館はホテルと違うのですか？

The *ryokan* is a traditional Japanese inn. Many of them are wooden structures and are located in areas with hot springs, so you can enjoy the very "Japanese" atmosphere.

旅館は日本の伝統的な宿です。その多くは木造建築で温泉地にあり、"和"の雰囲気を堪能できます。

□ wooden structure
木造建築
□ atmosphere
名 雰囲気

There are open-air baths and indoor big baths where you can enjoy bathing in a spacious space not possible at home.

露天風呂や屋内の大浴場があり、自宅では体験できない広々とした空間での入浴が楽しめます。

Some inns don't have any indoor baths.

部屋に内風呂がない旅館もあります。

You can check in in the afternoon, and enjoy the hot springs.

午後にチェックインして温泉を楽しみます。

Most places include dinner and breakfast, and traditional Japanese food is usually served at dinner.

一泊二食の設定になっていることが多く、夕食には伝統的な日本食が供されることが一般的です。

What are the rooms like at a *ryokan*?
旅館の部屋は何か特徴がありますか？

Many *ryokan* will have tea service with a Japanese tea set and local snacks.

多くの旅館の客室には、日本茶のティーセットとご当地の銘菓がお茶うけとして用意されています。

How about taking a tea break after you enter your room and organize your luggage?

お部屋に入って荷物をおろしたら、これで一息入れてはいかがでしょう。

In your room, you'll find *yukata* that you can wear as nightclothes.

部屋着兼寝巻として着用する浴衣が置いてあります。

Haori and *tanzen* jackets are sometimes added as outerwear in the cold season.

寒い季節の上着として、羽織や丹前が添えらえていることもあります。

☐ open-air bath
露天風呂

☐ spacious
形 広々とした

☐ local snacks
ご当地の銘菓

☐ outerwear
名 上着

● You can walk around the corridors and banquet halls in the *yukata*.

浴衣は、旅館内の廊下や宴会場などで着て歩くことができます。

□ corridor 名 廊下
□ banquet hall
宴会場

● In hot spring town, you can even go out wearing your *yukata*.

なお、温泉街では浴衣で外出することも可能です。

□ hot spring town
温泉街

Are there different types of inns?

旅館には種類がありますか？

● In addition to hot spring inns, there are also *ryokan* (commercial lodgings) used mainly by business people and students on school trips.

温泉旅館のほかに、主に都市部においてビジネスや修学旅行に利用される旅館（商人宿）というのもあります。

□ school trip
名 修学旅行

● Some *ryokan* in hot springs don't serve meals, that is, they are "self-catering inns" where you cook by yourself.

温泉地にある旅館の中には、食事の用意がない、つまり自分で料理をする「自炊旅館」というのがあります。

□ self-catering
自炊

● Many people visit the hot springs and stay for a long time to improve their health.

療養のために温泉を訪れる湯治客を中心に、長期で利用する人が多いです。

□ improve one's
health 療養する

● Hot springs have various health benefits, so how about giving it a try?

温泉にはいろいろな効能がありますので、一度チェックしてみてはいかがでしょう？

□ health benefit
効能

温水洗浄便座
Cleansing Toilet Seats with Water Spray

 02

「ウォシュレット」はTOTOが販売する温水洗浄便座の商品名（登録商標）です。一般名詞としては「温水洗浄便座」と言います。

英語で言うと？ --

自動で：**automatically**　便座：**toilet seat**　洋式便器：**western-style toilet**　普

及率：**adoption rate**　洗浄する：**cleanse**　和式トイレ：**Japanese-style toilet**

Photo: クロッシングさんによる写真 AC からの写真

What's a washlet?
ウォシュレットってどんなものですか？

It's a device for a toilet which has various functions.

色々な機能がついた洋式便器の装置です。

☐ device
　名 装置；機器
☐ toilet　名 便器
☐ function　名 機能
● 外国人の多くは、温水洗浄便座＝ washlet と認識しているので、こう聞かれることが多いです。

70

- It has functions to wash and dry your bottom, and heat the toilet seat, among other things.

  お尻を洗う、乾かす、便座を温めるなどの機能が付いています。

- There are also newer ones that automatically raise the toilet lid, and flush when you stand up.

  他にも、自動的に便座の蓋が開閉したり、立つと自動的に便器を洗浄するなど進化したものもあります。

Have Japanese people been using them for a long time?

日本人は昔から温水洗浄便座を使っているの？

- In the past, Japanese people used squat toilets, but in the 1970s Western-style toilets started to proliferate and became mainstream.

  昔はしゃがんで使う和式トイレが主流でしたが、1970年代に洋式トイレが普及し始めて以来洋式トイレが主流となりました。

- In 1980, a commercial became a hot topic and recognition increased, and it gradually spread to ordinary households.

  1980年に入り、CMが話題となり認知度が上がり、徐々に一般家庭に普及して行きました。

- The current ownership rate of electronic bidets is said to be about 80%.

  現在の温水洗浄便座の普及率は約80％と言われています。

文化

How much do they cost?
いくらくらいで買えるの？

● Electronic bidets that attach to existing toilets for home use can be purchased at home electronics stores for around 20,000 to 70,000 yen.

家庭用の既存の便器に取り付けるものは、2万円～7万円前後で家電量販店などで購入できます。

□ existing
形 現存する；現在の
□ home electronics
家電

● The market price for a toilet with an electronic bidet is about 200,000 to 300,000 yen.

便器そのものは20万から30万円ぐらいが一般的な相場です。

□ market price
市場価格

● You can install it yourself, but if you ask a contractor, you will be charged a separate fee.

自分でも取り付けることができますが、業者に頼むと取り付け費用が別途かかります。

□ install
動 インストールする；設置する
□ contractor
名 請負業者

Question 1 にある「ウォシュレット」は、TOTOの商品名であり**登録商標 (registered trademark)** なのですが、今や日本はもとより、世界的に普及・定着しているため、他社製品を含めた温水洗浄便座全般のことを指して「ウォシュレット」という言葉が使われるほどになっています。

THEME 28 自動販売機
Vending Machines

28

文
化

最も身近でメインジャンルと言える飲料の自販機以外に、高速のSAなどに
ある食品の自販機などもご案内すると喜ばれるのではないでしょうか。

英語で言うと？

清涼飲料水：**soft drink**　コインロッカー：**coin-operated locker**　券売機：**ticket-vending machine**　両替機：**money exchange machine**　日用雑貨：**daily use commodities**　高速のサービスエリア：**highway rest stop**

Photo: Licensed under Public Domain via Wikimedia Commons / Flickr　帰属：heriheri

Why are there so many vending machines in Japan?
どうして日本には自動販売機が多いのですか？

● One reason why there are more vending machines than overseas is that Japan is safe.

海外に比べて自販機が多い理由は、日本の治安の良さが理由の一つです。

□ vending machine
　自動販売機

73

Vending machines are rarely vandalized.

自販機が荒らされるという犯罪は滅多に起こりません。

Due to the high population density, demand inevitably increases, and so does the number of vending machines, especially in the city center.

人口密度が高いため、必然的に需要が高まり、特に都心部では自販機の台数が多くなります。

Because summer in Japan is hot, many people need to rehydrate on the go.

日本の夏は暑いので、水分補給を外出先でもするため多くの人に必要とされています。

□ rarely	副 めったに〜ない；まれに
□ vandalized	動 破壊する；いたずらする
□ population density	人口密度
□ demand	名 需要
□ inevitably	副 必然的に；必ず
□ rehydrate	動 水分補給する
□ on the go	出先で

What kind of vending machines are there besides soft-drink vending machines?

ジュース以外にどんな自販機がありますか？

In rest stops on highways, there are vending machines for things like hamburgers, fries and *ramen*.

高速道路のサービスエリアなどでは、ハンバーガーやポテト、ラーメンなどの自販機があります。

Cigarettes can be purchased at vending machines, but an IC card called TASPO, which is only issued for adults, is required.

タバコも自販機で買えますが、成人のみに発行されるTASPOと呼ばれるICカードが必要です。

There are not so many of them, but gifts such as bouquets and wedding rings can also be bought at vending machines.

たくさんはありませんが、花束や結婚指輪といった贈り物も自販機で買うことができます。

□ rest stop	休憩のための停車；パーキング [サービス] エリア
□ fries	名 フライドポテト
□ issue	動 公表する；発行する
□ require	動 〜を必要とする
□ bouquet	名 花束

What other roles do they play?

他にどんな役割を果たしますか？

🙂 Vending machines have a sticker with an address on it, so you can see where you are.

自販機には住所の書かれたステッカーが貼られていて、自分が今どこにいるかわかります。

🙂 It's not only for when you get lost, but also so that when you call an ambulance or the police, you can tell where you are.

迷った時だけではなく、救急車や警察を呼ぶときに自分の居場所を知らせることができるようになっています。

🙂 Some vending machines allow you to drink for free in the event of a disaster.

自販機によっては災害時に飲料が無料で飲めるようになるものもあります。

□ allow 動 許す；考慮に入れる

🙂 There are over 10,000 machines nationwide.

全国に1万台以上あります。

□ nationwide
副 全国的に
形 全国的な

生みたての卵が買える、「卵の自販機」！ さすがに商品が落下する方式ではなく、コインロッカーのようなシステムになっている。

Photo: iStockphoto.com / gyro

75

食品サンプル
Model Food

⬇ 29

お寿司や天ぷらなどの和食を中心に、お土産としても人気の高い食品サンプル。機会があればぜひ制作体験にお連れしたいですね！

英語で言うと？ -

ストラップ：**strap**　制作体験：**try making (something)**　蝋：**wax**
シリコン：**silicon**　合成樹脂：**synthetic resin**　型：**mold**

Photo: Licensed under Public Domain via Wikimedia Commons / Flickr

How are display models of food made?
食品サンプルはどうやってできているんですか？

😊 Basically, they are made using a synthetic resin such as wax or silicon.

基本的には、ろうやシリコンなどの合成樹脂などを使って作ります。

☐ synthetic resin
　合成樹脂
☐ wax　名 ろう
☐ silicon　名 シリコン

A mold is made using the actual food, and silicon is poured into the mold.

食品の実物を使って型をとり、その型にシリコンなどを流して成形します。

Finally, they use an airbrush or brush to color and finish it.

最後にエアブラシや筆を使って色付けして仕上げます。

That's where the craftsperson shows off their skill.

ここは職人の腕の見せ所と言えるでしょう。

Where can I try making one?
どんなところで体験できますか？

You can experience it at companies that actually produce food models, and at shops that sell food models.

実際に食品サンプルを制作している会社や食品サンプルを販売しているお店で体験できます。

Sometimes events are held at places like museums in sightseeing spots.

観光地の美術館などでもイベントとして行なっていることがあります。

Depending on what you make, you can participate for around 1,000 to 3,000 yen.

作る作品によりますが、1000円～3000円前後で参加することができます。

Individual vegetables are cheap, and elaborate items like parfaits are expensive.

野菜単品などは安く、パフェなど手の込んだものは高くなります。

□ mold 名 型
□ actual
　形 現実の；実際の

□ airbrush
　名 エアブラシ
□ craftsperson
　名 職人；名人

□ show off
　見せつける

□ produce
　動 作り出す

□ participate
　動 参加する
□ individual
　形 個人の；個別の
□ elaborate
　形 複雑な

文化

What can you make?
どんなものが作れるの？

● Vegetables like lettuce, and tempura, which are easy even for beginners to make are standard.

初心者でも作りやすいレタスなどの野菜や天ぷらなどが定番です。

● Sweets such as macaroons, pudding a la mode, and cream puffs are popular with women.

女性にはマカロン、プリンアラモード、シュークリームなどのスイーツが人気があります。

● You can take home a model as is, or have it made into a key holder or accessory and take it home as a souvenir.

食品サンプルのまま、もしくはキーホルダーやアクセサリーにして作った作品をお土産として持って帰ることができます。

□ macaroon
名 マカロン
□ pudding a la mode
プリンアラモード
□ cream puff
シュークリーム

レタスの食品サンプル制作
過程のひとコマ

Photo: 俺の空 / PIXTA (ピクスタ)

78

THEME 30

高架下の飲み屋
Bars under the Elevated Tracks (*koukashita*)

 30

文化

特に都市部のガード下を利用した施設はちょっとした非日常空間を味わえるので"探検"気分を楽しんでもらえるおすすめスポットです。

超人気スポット！ 有楽町のガード下

英語で言うと？

高架：**elevated**　耐震補強工事：**seismic reinforcement**
再開発：**redevelopment**　改装：**refurbishment**　洗練された：**sophisticated**
昔ながらの：**retro feel**

写真提供：(公財) 東京観光財団

What kind of place is "koukashita"?
「高架下」とはどのような場所ですか？

For reasons such as the site is narrow, long, and noisy, *koukashita* were mainly used for parking lots and warehouses.

高架下は、敷地が細長い、騒音がうるさい……などの理由から駐車場や倉庫に利用されがちな場所でした。

□ site　名 敷地
□ parking lot
　駐車場
□ warehouse
　名 倉庫

Recently, the number of railway companies looking to heighten its appeal as a facility has increased.

最近では、施設としての魅力を高めようとする鉄道会社が増えてきました。

□ railway company
鉄道会社
□ heighten
動 高くする
□ appeal 名 魅力
□ facility 名 施設

Things such as seismic reinforcement work on elevated tracks and station refurbishment sparked the use of the area under the elevated tracks.

高架の耐震補強工事や駅の改装などが、高架下活用のきっかけです。

□ seismic 形 地震の
□ reinforcement
名 補強 (すること)
□ refurbishment
名 改修
□ spark 動 〜の火付け役となる

What kinds of shops are there under the elevated tracks?

高架下はどのようなお店が入っていますか？

One cool facility after another has opened, overturning the dark image it used to have.

しゃれた施設が次々にオープンし、かつての暗いイメージをくつがえしています。

□ overturn
動 ひっくり返す

In addition to cafes and galleries, there are some places where things such as fitness gyms and nursery schools are opening.

カフェやギャラリーのほか、フィットネスジムや保育園などが入っている場所もあります。

□ in addition to
〜に加えて

□ nursery school
保育園

Each area has its own characteristics, like the cool area of Meguro, the sophisticated Oimachi, and Yurakucho, which has a retro feel.

おしゃれな中目黒や、洗練された大井町、レトロな有楽町など、地域ごとに特徴があります。

□ characteristic
名 特性

□ sophisticated
形 洗練された
□ retro 形 レトロの

Where are the famous Japanese-style pub spots under the elevated tracks?

有名な高架下の居酒屋スポットはどこですか？

The area under the elevated tracks connecting JR Yurakucho and Shimbashi Stations was built over 100 years ago.

JR有楽町駅〜新橋駅をつなぐ高架下は今から100年以上前に作られたものです。

As the seats are small and the distance from other customers is short, it naturally stimulates conversation.

座席は狭く、他のお客さんとの距離も近いため、自然と会話も弾みます。

Popular areas under the elevated tracks include the stretch between Ueno and Akihabara, as well as Kanda, and Nakameguro.

上野〜秋葉原間や神田、中目黒なども、人気のある高架下です。

□ connect
動 〜をつなぐ

□ customer 名 顧客
□ naturally
副 当然 (ながら)
□ stimulate
〜を刺激 [奨励] する

□ stretch 名 伸びる
程度 [範囲]；期間

東京の高架下と言われて絶対に外せないスポットの一つ、上野アメ横！ 高架下のディープな飲み屋を攻略するもよし、お得な食品類を買い求めるもよし！

Photo: みっくすさんによる写真 AC からの写真

81

THEME 31

のれんの出し入れ
The Custom of Taking Shop Curtains (*noren*) in and out

 31

「のれん」の由来や意味など、改めて問われると意外と知らないこともあるのではないでしょうか。異文化交流的にも面白いトピックでは？

英語で言うと？ ---

目隠し：**screen** 繁盛店：**thriving shop** 汚い：**dirty** 営業中：**be open** 片づける：**put away** 慣用句：**idiom**

Photo: Fast&Slow / PIXTA (ピクスタ)

What are "noren"?
のれんとはなんですか？

🔵 It is a fabric that prevents wind and light from coming directly into the shop, and serves as a screen.

屋内に直接、風や光が入るのを防いだり、目隠しとして使われる布です。

☐ fabric 名 布
☐ prevent 動 防ぐ
☐ directly 副 直接
☐ serve
　　動 役目を果たす

82

◉ Before the war, as customers would leave, there was the custom of having them wipe their dirty hands on the *noren*.

戦前、客が帰る際、汚れた手をのれんで拭いていく、という習慣がありました。

◉ For this reason, shops with dirtier *noren* were said to be "thriving shops."

そのため、のれんが汚れている店ほど「繁盛しているお店」と言われていました。

☐ thriving
形 繁盛している

Do they put the *noren* out when they open shops?

開店の時にのれんを出すのですか？

◉ *Noren* have various purposes and messages, and when they are put out, it signals that a shop is open.

のれんには様々な目的やメッセージがあり、のれんを出すことが「営業中」の合図になります。

☐ various
形 さまざまな
☐ purpose 名 目的
☐ signal
動 伝える；示す

◉ This is why the first thing a shop does when it is closing is to put the *noren* away.

そのため、お店を閉店する場合は、まずのれんを片づけます。

◉ The idiom "taking down the *noren*" incorporates the meaning, "going out of business."

「のれんをおろす」という慣用句には「廃業する」という意味があります。

☐ idiom
名 熟語；慣用句
☐ incorporate
動 ～を組み込む；包含する
☐ go out of business
廃業する

Are *noren* known as fabric signs?

のれんは「布の看板」と言われているのですか？

Back in the Muromachi period, in order to make known each shop's name and type, they began including proprietary designs.

室町時代になると、店舗ごとに屋号や業種などを知らしめるため、独自のデザインを入れるようになりました。

At the time, there were few people who could read the characters, so most *noren* bore things such as animal and plant patterns.

当時は文字を読める人が少なかったので、動物や植物などの文様を、のれんの中心に入れました。

The type of shop was evident by the color of the *noren* — for instance, merchants were scarlet or indigo, while confectionery shops and drugstores were white and brown.

商家は緋色や藍色、お菓子屋や薬屋は白色や茶色のように、色によって業種が分かれていました。

□ period　名 期間
□ in order to
　〜するために
□ proprietary
　形 所有者の；私有の

□ character　名 文字
□ bear
　動 有する；抱く
□ pattern　名 文様

□ evident　形 明白な
□ for instance
　例えば
□ merchant
　名 商人；業者
□ scarlet　形 緋色の
　名 緋色
□ indigo　形 藍色の
　名 藍色
□ confectionery
　名 菓子製造；菓子類

布ではなく縄を使った縄暖簾も。居酒屋などでよく使われているため、「縄暖簾で一杯やろう」など、居酒屋そのものを指す表現もある

カラオケ
THEME 32
Karaoke

 32

karaokeとしてすでに英単語にもなっているカラオケですが、アメリカなどとは違った、グループ単位や個人での楽しみ方も一緒にご案内しましょう。

英語で言うと？

空っぽの：**empty**　料金システム：**fee structure**　ワンドリンク制：**one-drink minimum**　一般料金：**basic fee**　会員料金：**member's fee**
（飲食物の）持ち込み：**bringing in food and drink**

Photo: gimyzr さんによる写真 AC からの写真

Was *karaoke* born in Japan?
カラオケは日本で生まれたの？

Karaoke is short for "karappo", which means "empty" and "orchestra", and it means an orchestral recording with no vocals.

カラオケの「から」は「空っぽ」オケは「オーケストラ」の略で、歌の入っていないオーケストラを意味する日本語です。

☐ empty　形 空の
☐ orchestral
　　形 オーケストラの

85

It became popular in Japan around 1970, and when the *karaoke* box was invented everyone was able to enjoy it.

1970年ごろから日本で流行りだし、「カラオケボックス」の登場で誰もが楽しめるようになりました。

□ invent 動 ～を発明する；考案する

Nowadays, more and more people are enjoying *karaoke*, not only in Japan, but all over the world, starting with Asia.

今では日本だけではなく、アジア圏をはじめ、世界中でカラオケを楽しむ人が増えています。

How do people have fun in *karaoke* boxes?
カラオケボックスではどんな楽しみ方がありますか？

Since prices are set comparatively low during the daytime, it seems that they are often used by groups of elderly people and mom friends.

昼間は比較的安い値段で設定されているため、高齢者の集まりやママ友同士で利用されることが多いようです。

□ daytime 名 昼間
□ elderly 形 年配の

There is also a service called "hitori karaoke" that can be used by one person. You sing with headphones in a small box.

１人でも利用できる「一人カラオケ」というサービスもあります。小さなボックスの中でヘッドフォーンをして歌います。

It can be used if you are embarrassed to be heard by others, or to practice before going to *karaoke* with someone.

他の人に聞かれたら恥ずかしい人や、誰かとカラオケに行く前の練習に利用したりします。

□ embarrassed 形 恥ずかしい

There are also *karaoke* boxes that offers a full range of food services, so you can enjoy the food even if you are not good at singing.

料理のサービスが充実しているカラオケボックスもあるので、歌が苦手でも、お料理を楽しむことができます。

□ full range 全種類そろった

What functions do *karaoke* machines have?

カラオケの機械にはどんな機能があるんですか？

You can change the key and tempo. There is also a harmonizing function.

キーの高さを変えたり、テンポなどを変えたりすることができます。ハモリ機能などもあります。

☐ harmonize
動 〜に和声 [ハーモニー] をつける

Since the scoring functions are getting more and more sophisticated, you can compete with your friends over the high score and find out how highly you scored compared to everyone else in Japan.

採点機能はどんどん充実しているため、高得点を友人同士で競ったり、自分の歌の点数が全国で何位かを知ることができます。

☐ compete
動 競争する
☐ score
動 (〜を) 得点する

Songs that play the real singer's music video on the screen or explain the choreography are also popular.

本物の歌手のミュージックビデオが画面に流れたり、曲の振り付けを解説してくれる曲も人気があります。

☐ choreography
名 振り付け

「英語の歌を歌いたいけどなかなか難しい…」と思っている方におすすめなのは、第一興商という会社のNipponglish® という、洋楽をカラオケで歌うための便利な仕組みです。カラオケの画面に出る英語の歌詞のカタカナルビが実際の英語の音に近いものになっていて、これを使うと英語が苦手な人でもネイティブライクな発音で歌うことができます。

THEME 33 アニメ
Anime

33

日本が世界に誇るコンテンツの1つがアニメであることは間違いありません。そのテーマや対象年齢の幅広さに、驚かれるかもしれません。

東京工芸大学　杉並アニメーションミュージアムのエントランス

英語で言うと？ -

アニメ映画：**animated film**　原作漫画：**original manga**　人気がある：**popular**
老若男女：**men and women of all ages**　声優：**voice actor**　コラボカフェ：
collaborative cafe

Are there tourist spots that are mentioned in Japanese anime?

日本のアニメに触れられる観光スポットはありますか？

There is a facility in Tokyo's Suginami Ward called Tokyo Polytechnic University Suginami Animation Museum.

東京の杉並区に、「東京工芸大学　杉並アニメーションミュージアム」という施設があります。

There, you can enjoy all aspects of Japanese anime, from its history to its future.

□ aspect 名 角度；方位

そこでは「日本のアニメの歴史」から「これからのアニメ」まで幅広く、日本のアニメについて楽しみながら学ぶことができます。

There are also opportunities to participate in dubbing, as well as creating anime through coloring and editing.

□ dubbing 名 アフレコ

アフレコや色塗りや編集などのアニメ制作を体験できるコーナーもありますよ。

Since when has anime been popular?
日本のアニメ人気はいつから？

It became popular in Japan starting in 1963, thanks to Osamu Tezuka's "Astro Boy".

1963年、手塚治虫の「鉄腕アトム」によってアニメ人気が日本に広がり始めました。

Pokemon has become loved by children not just in Japan, but all over the world, and the video games and merchandise are also popular.

□ merchandise 動 (商品などを) 売買する 名 商品；品物

ポケットモンスターが日本だけではなく、世界中の子供に愛されるようになり、ゲームやグッズなども人気があります。

At the 75th Academy Awards, "Spirited Away", directed by Hayao Miyazaki, won Best Animated Feature, and the quality of Japanese animation was praised.

□ direct 動 (映画や舞台を) 監督する
□ praise 動 〜をほめる；たたえる

第75回 アカデミー賞にて、宮崎駿監督の「千と千尋の神隠し」が長編アニメーション映画賞を受賞したことで、日本のアニメのクオリティの高さが評価されました。

文化

89

Why are anime and manga popular with adults as well?

どうして日本のアニメや漫画は大人にも人気があるのですか？

They have a wide variety of themes and genres that adults can also enjoy.

テーマが幅広く、大人も楽しめるジャンルが多く存在するからです。

There is content such as business, gourmet food and medicine that adults can enjoy.

ビジネスものやグルメ、医療ものなどは大人が楽しめる内容になっています。

Even in works aimed at children, there are story developments that adults can also enjoy.

子供向けの作品でも、大人も楽しめるようなストーリー展開になっています。

□ genre
名 ジャンル；分野

□ content
名 (本や雑誌、芸術作品などの) 内容

□ gourmet food
グルメ食品

□ medicine
名 医学；薬物療法

□ aim at ｜〜に狙いを定める

□ development
名 発展；進行

東京工芸大学 杉並アニメーションミュージアム
日本のアニメ全般を紹介している日本初のアニメーション博物館。
アニメ好きにはたまらないイベントやワークショップがもりだくさん !!

開館時間 10:00 〜 18:00 (入館は 17:30 まで)
休館日 月曜日 (祝祭日の場合はその翌日)
入館料 無料
住所 〒 167-0043 東京都杉並区上荻 3-29-5 杉並会館 3 階
TEL 03-3396-1510
FAX 03-3396-1530
ホームページ https://sam.or.jp/
公式 Twitter @suginami_sam

● 休館日など最新の情報は、ホームページやツイッターなどでチェックしてください

THEME 34 聖地巡礼
Holy Pilgrimage

作品世界に浸かり、実際にモデルとなった場所や建物を訪れるために訪日する外国人も多くいます（むしろ彼らのほうが詳しいなんてことも！）。

映画『君の名は。』の聖地として有名な、東京都新宿区の須賀神社の階段

英語で言うと？

聖地：**sacred place**　　巡礼：**pilgrimage**　　画角：**viewing angle**　　自撮り：**selfie**
登場人物：**character**　　実写映画：**live-action film**

Photo: ポコポコさんによる写真 AC からの写真

What is a holy pilgrimage?
聖地巡礼って何？

It is actually visiting locations that were used as a basis for popular anime and *manga*.

人気のアニメや漫画のモデルとなった舞台を実際に訪れることです。

□ holy pilgrimage
　神聖な巡礼（の旅）

□ actually　副 実際に
□ location　名 場所
□ basis
　名 土台；基礎

91

🟢 The places and buildings that the anime was based on are called "holy places".

モデルとなった場所や建物は「聖地」と呼ばれます。

☐ holy place　聖地

🟢 Some fans do "holy pilgrimages" to the sets of live-action movies and dramas as well as anime.

アニメだけではなく、実写の映画やドラマの「聖地巡礼」をするファンもいます。

☐ live-action
動画の；生の

Where are particularly famous locations?
特に有名なところはどこ？

🟢 The original holy place is said to be Tarou Shrine in Okayama Prefecture, which appeared in the comic "Tenchi Muyo!

元祖の聖地は漫画の「天地無用！」に出てきた岡山県の太老神社と言われています。

☐ particularly
副 特に；非常に

☐ original　形 最初の

🟢 Hida City, Gifu Prefecture, which was the setting for the movie "Your Name", sparked the trend.

映画『君の名は。』の舞台となった、岐阜県飛騨市がブームの火付け役になりました。

☐ setting
名 拝啓；設定

🟢 A small railroad crossing near the Enoshima Electric Railway's Kamakura High School Station in Kanagawa appeared in the popular anime "Slam Dunk", and is known overseas as a holy place.

神奈川県の江ノ電「鎌倉高校前駅」近くの小さな踏切は人気アニメ『スラムダンク』に登場し、海外にも聖地として知られています。

☐ overseas
副 海外に

What do everyone do in holy places?
聖地ではみんな何をするのですか？

They take photos at the same angle as was shown in the movie.

映画と同じようなアングルで写真を撮ったりします。

At restaurants, they order the same food as the characters, and take pictures.

飲食店では、登場人物と同じ食べ物を注文して写真を撮ったりします。

There are people who participate in tours organized by travel agencies, and travel around the country.

旅行会社が企画するツアーに参加して、各地を巡る人もいます。

☐ angle 名 角度

☐ participate in
～に参加する
☐ organize
動 (イベントを) 企画
する

飛騨古川駅もまた、映画
『君の名は。』の聖地とし
て注目されたスポット

Photo: igamania さんによる写真 AC からの写真

忍者カフェ
Ninja Cafes

 35

伊賀甲賀の忍者の里はもちろんですが、都心部にある忍者をコンセプトにした飲食店で、「Ninja」気軽に楽しんでもらうのもおすすめです。

英語で言うと？ -

武道：**martial arts**　忍術：**ninja arts**　世界観：**world view**　手裏剣：**throwing stars**　〜の扮装をする：**dress as 〜**　堪能する：**fully enjoy**

Photo: iStockphoto.com / kuppa_rock

What kind of place is a *ninja* cafe?
忍者カフェってどんなところですか？

It's a cafe based on the concept of *ninja*, and the staff serve you in *ninja* costumes.

忍者をコンセプトとしたカフェで、スタッフは忍者の衣装で接客します。

☐ concept
名 概念；コンセプト

🥷 Most of them charge by the hour, and you pay a basic fee first, and then incur additional charges depending on the length of your stay.

大抵、時間制料金になっていて、最初に基本料金を支払い、その後滞在時間に応じて追加料金が発生します。

🥷 The interior of the cafe is Japanese-style, so you can immerse yourself in the world of *ninja*.

店内は和をイメージした空間になって、忍者の世界に浸れるようになっています。

🥷 They are also popular with *ninja*-loving foreigners.

忍者好きの外国人にも人気があります。

What services are available?
どんなサービスがありますか？

🥷 There are also cafes where you can play games like *shuriken* darts for an additional fee.

追加料金を支払うと、手裏剣ダーツなどゲームができるお店もあります。

🥷 You can dress up as a *ninja* and take a commemorative photo with the staff.

忍者の扮装をして、スタッフと一緒に記念撮影をすることができます。

🥷 There are also performances by the *ninja* staff such as board breaking and dances.

板割りや演舞など忍者スタッフによるパフォーマンスなどもあります。

□ incur
動 (費用などを) 負担する
□ additional
形 追加の
□ charge 名 料金

□ interior
形 内部の；室内の
□ immerse
動 浸す；没頭させる

□ commemorative photo 記念写真

What is a *ninja* restaurant like?
忍者レストランはどんなものですか？

It's a restaurant where you can enjoy the world of *ninja*, and staff dressed as *ninja* bring you food.

忍者の世界を堪能できるレストランで、忍者の格好をしたスタッフがお料理などを運んでくれます。

There are restaurants where *ninja* magic shows and performances take place.

忍者のマジックやパフォーマンスが行われるレストランがあります。

There are restaurants where you can rent out *ninja* costumes, and you can dine in the *ninja* costumes and take photos.

忍者コスチュームの貸し出しをしているレストランでは、忍者の衣装で食事をしたり写真撮影ができます。

☐ dine 動 食事をする

Hood (頭巾)
Besides hiding the face, this could be used as a bandage or a rope to climb walls.
顔を隠す以外にも、包帯や壁を登るロープに利用できた

Coat (上着)
It had a lot of pockets on the inside.
内側にはたくさんのポケットがついていた

***Hakama* pants (袴)**
This type of loose clothing made it easy to move.
作りに余裕があるので、動きやすかった

Leg wraps (脚絆)
These were used to keep grass and other things from getting inside their shoes.
靴の中に草などが入らないように巻いた

THEME 36

漫画喫茶・ネットカフェ 🔽 36
Manga Cafes / Internet Cafes

文化

漫画やインターネットが使える"漫喫""ネカフェ"は、シャワー設備や防音付の個室など、より快適に、多様に、日々進化しています。

英語で言うと？

読み放題：**unlimited reading**　飲み放題：**all-you-can-drink**　24時間営業：**open 24 hours**　個室：**private room**　防音の：**soundproof**　終電：**last train**

Photo: Graphs / PIXTA (ピクスタ)

What kinds of things can you do at a "mangakissa," or *manga* cafe?

漫画喫茶はどんなことができるの？

😊 You can read all the *manga* and magazines you want, they have all-you-can-drink beverages, and are almost all open 24 hours a day.

漫画や雑誌などが読み放題、飲み物も飲み放題でほとんどが24時間営業です。

☐ beverage
名 飲み物

97

There are also shops where you can enjoy online games or *karaoke*.

ほかにオンラインゲームやカラオケなどができる店もあります。

 At large-scale shops, you can play billiards, table tennis, or darts, and you can even take a shower.

大規模な店では、ビリヤード・卓球・ダーツなどもでき、シャワーを浴びることもできます。

 About how much does it cost?
料金はどのくらいかかる？

 Fees are time-based, and you can extend your time by paying an additional fee.

時間制で料金を払いますが、追加料金を払えば時間延長もできます。

☐ time-based
時間ベースの
☐ extend
動 伸ばす；延長する；伸びる

 There are also shops that have VIP rooms, soundproof private rooms with locks, and private rooms that families can use.

VIP室や防音で鍵つきの個室、ファミリーで使える個室がある店もあります。

☐ soundproof
形 防音の

 How long have there been *mangakissa*?
漫画喫茶はいつどこで始まったの？

 It is said that they got their start in 1977 when the owner of a coffee shop in Aichi Prefecture, who loved *manga*, placed many of them around his shop.

1977年ごろに愛知県の喫茶店で漫画好きなオーナーがたくさんの漫画を店に置いたことが始まりと言われています。

 Aichi Prefecture has lots of coffee shops, so they leave many *manga* around the shop in order to attract customers.

愛知県は喫茶店が多いので、お客さんを呼ぶために漫画をたくさん置いたようです。

☐ attract
動 引き付ける；魅了する

98

🙂 That particular coffee shop is no longer operating, but the owner is said to have started Japan's first *mangakissa*.

現在はその喫茶店は営業していませんが、そのオーナーが日本初の漫画喫茶を始めたのだと言われています。

文化

What do you do at an internet cafe?
ネットカフェって何するところ？

🙂 It's a cafe where you can use the internet for free if you pay the fee. In Japan, we call them "nekafe".

料金を払えばインターネットを無料で使えるカフェです。日本では「ネカフェ」と略されたりします。

🙂 The main purpose is to use the internet, but there are people who go there to read magazines or *manga*, or for all-you-can-drink drinks or all-you-can-eat ice cream.

メインはネットを利用することですが、雑誌や漫画を読んだり、ドリンクの飲み放題やソフトクリームの食べ放題などを目当てに来店する人もいます。

☐ all-you-can-drink
飲み放題の

🙂 Most of them are open 24 hours, so sometimes people who miss the last train pass the time there until the first train the next morning.

24時間営業の店舗がほとんどなので、終電を逃した人たちが始発まで時間を潰すのに利用することもあります。

☐ pass the time
ひまをつぶす

What's it like inside?
店内はどんな風ですか？

🙂 You enter after paying the base fee at the reception desk. Usually you need proof of identity to use one.

入り口の受付で基本料金などを支払ってから店内に入ります。利用するためには大抵本人確認証が必要になります。

There are partitioned counters and private rooms that can be used by one person, friends or couples. Many cafes have women-only areas that are easy for women to use.

仕切られたカウンターか、個室を1人、もしくは友達同士やカップルなどで利用することができます。女性も利用しやすいように女性専用エリアを設けているカフェも多いです。

□ partitioned
形 分割した

□ women-only
女性専用

The chair can be reclined or laid flat, so you can relax. Some stores offer massage chairs.

椅子はリクライニングやフラットにすることができるので、ゆったりくつろぐことができます。中にはマッサージチェアを提供する店舗もあります。

□ recline
動 寄りかかる；後ろに倒れる

What other services are available?
他にはどんなサービスを受けられますか？

Some facilities are equipped with showers, so some tourists use them instead of hotels.

シャワーが併設されている施設もあるので、ホテルがわりに利用する観光客もいます。

□ be equipped with
〜を備えている

There are also facilities where you can play billiards, darts and *karaoke*.

ビリヤードやダーツ、カラオケなどをすることができる施設もあります。

There are cafes where you can bring your own food, and at cafes that have business partnerships with food delivery services, you can order in.

食べ物の持ち込みがOKなカフェや、飲食の宅配サービスと業務提携しているカフェでは出前もとることができます。

□ business partnership
事業提携

THEME 37 猫カフェ
Cat Cafes

 37

猫ブームで「猫カフェ」もまた賑わっており、海外からのお客様も増加傾向です。お店ごとのシステムを把握し、きちんとご案内しましょう。

英語で言うと？

放し飼い：**let run free**　靴をぬぐ：**take off one's shoes**　癒される：**be healed**
追加注文：**additional order**　保護猫：**rescued cat**　里親：**foster parents**

Photo: Fast&Slow / PIXTA (ピクスタ)

What do you do at a cat cafe?
猫カフェは何をするところですか？

Cats are kept free in the cafe and you can pet them as much as you like while drinking coffee.

□ pet
動 ～をかわいがる

カフェの店内に猫が放し飼いにされていて、コーヒーなどを飲みながら自由に触ったりすることができます。

101

😺 It's a place for cat lovers and those who can't keep cats at home to be soothed by cats.

猫が好きな人や猫を家で飼えない人が猫に癒されるための場所です。

☐ soothe
動 〜を安心させる；安心させる

😺 You can take pictures of them, or spend your free time just watching them.

写真を撮ったり、ただ眺めたり自由な過ごし方ができます。

☐ lap 名 膝

😺 Most shops prohibit holding the cats, but it's OK if they jump into your lap.

ほとんどのお店は抱っこ禁止ですが、猫が自分から膝に乗ってくるのはOKです。

What are the cafe systems like?

お店のシステムはどうなっているのですか？

😺 It depends on the cafe, but basically, you have to pay an entrance fee or the hourly fee before entering the store.

お店によって違いますが、基本的には先に入場料もしくは時間制のコース料金を支払ってから入店します。

😺 Many cafes let you take off your shoes to relax.

多くのお店は靴を脱いでくつろぐことできます。

😺 You may need to order one drink separately from the entrance fee.

入場料とは別途ワンドリンクを注文する必要がある場合もあります。

☐ separately
副 〜から切り離して；個別に

😺 You pay for additional orders when you leave the store.

追加注文などは退店時に支払います。

😺 There are also cafes where you can feed the cats treats.

猫におやつをあげられるカフェもあります。

☐ treat
名 もてなし；おやつ

☺ You can feed the cats a treat prepared by the store for around 300 yen.

300円前後でお店の用意したおやつを自分であげることができます。

What kinds of cat cafes are there?
どんな猫カフェがあるの？

☺ There are cat cafes that are restricted to certain types of cats, such as cats with short legs like munchkins.

マンチカンなど足の短い猫など、猫の種類を限定した猫カフェもあります。

☐ restrict
動 〜を限定する

☺ Some cafés have cats that are temporarily being kept and looking for foster parents, called "protected cats", and if you meet the requirements, you can also welcome your favorite cat to the family.

保護猫と呼ばれる一時的に保護されて里親を探している猫がいるカフェもあり、条件を満たせば、気に入った猫を家族として迎え入れることもできます。

☐ temporarily
副 一時的に
☐ foster parent
里親
☐ protected
形 保護された
☐ requirement
名 必需品；必要条件

☺ There are also cafes that are focused on food with plenty of sweets, and alcoholic drinks.

スイーツが充実していたり、アルコールを提供していたりと、料理などに力を入れているカフェもあります。

☐ be focuse on
〜に焦点を合わせている
☐ plenty of
たくさんの

Photo: あんみつ娘 / PIXTA (ピクスタ)

THEME 38 ハリネズミカフェ・フクロウカフェ 📥38
Hedgehog Cafes/Owl Cafes

猫以外の動物と触れ合えるカフェもあります。フクロウやハリネズミ以外に、小鳥のカフェや、数種の動物と触れ合えるカフェなどもあります。

英語で言うと？ -

手のひら：**palm of one's hand**　混んでいる：**crowded**　予約を受け付ける：**accept reservations**　バータイム：**bar time**　餌をやる：**feed**　貸し切り：**rent for private use**

Photo: ましろ / PIXTA (ピクスタ)

What kind of place is a hedgehog cafe?
ハリネズミカフェってどんなところですか？

😊 It's a cafe where you can encounter hedgehogs.

ハリネズミと触れ合うことができるカフェです。

😊 You can watch the hedgehogs while you drink coffee and eat sweets.

ハリネズミを眺めながらコーヒーを飲んだり、スイーツを食べたりできます。

☐ hedgehog
　名 ハリネズミ

☐ encounter
　動 (思いがけず) 出合う

104

Depending on the cafe, you can hold a hedgehog in the palm of your hand and take a photo together.

□ palm 名 手のひら

カフェによってはハリネズミを手のひらにのせたり、一緒に写真をとることができます。

What kind of system is it?
どんなシステムですか？

It depends on the cafe, but usually an hourly rate with one drink order.

□ hourly rate
時給；1時間あたりの料金

店ごとに異なりますがワンドリンク付の時間制になります。

The price is usually about 1,000 yen for 30 minutes or 2,000 yen for one hour.

料金はたいてい30分1000円、1時間2000円前後が多いです。

Popular cafes are crowded, so some take reservations.

□ reservation
名 予約

人気店は混んでいるので、予約可能なカフェもあります。

What kind of cafe is an owl cafe?
フクロウカフェってどんなカフェ？

It's a cafe where owls are kept free-range and you can interact with them.

□ free-range
放し飼いの
□ interact
動 (互いに) 作用する；交流する

フクロウが放し飼いにされていて、触れ合うことができるカフェです。

There are also cafes that sell owl-related items.

フクロウのグッズを扱っているカフェもあります。

There are also cafes that become bars at night. Cafes specializing in cilantro dishes have also become popular.

□ specialize
動 専攻する；〜を詳しく調べる；特殊化する
□ cilantro
名 コリアンダー；パクチー

夜はバータイムになるカフェもあり、お酒を飲んだり料理を楽しむことができます。パクチー料理などに特化したお店も話題になりました。

What can you do there?

どんなことができるの？

💬 Depending on the time, you can feed the owls.

時間によってはフクロウにえさやりをすることができます。

💬 You can take a commemorative photo with an owl on your hand or head. Some cafes charge extra.

手や頭にのせて記念写真をとることができます。別料金がかかるお店もあります。

☐ extra 副 余分に

💬 There are also cafes that you can rent for private use if you have enough people.

人数が集まれば、貸切できるカフェもあります。

☐ private use
私的利用

Photo: 38OWL03_pixta

Chapter 2

外国人がいちばん不思議に思う
日本のくらし・習慣

たんすやハンコ、お冷やや交番など、日本人のくらしにはおなじみのあれこれ、駐車場での車のとめかたやゲンかつぎのような独特の習慣について、簡単な英語で、基本は3ステップで、ご案内していきましょう！

DAILY LIFE
CUSTOM

ハンコ、印鑑
Hanko and *Inkan*

39

日本人のくらしにはお馴染みのハンコ・印鑑ですが、こういう習慣がない
国の人も多いです。どんな時に使うのか、英語で説明してみましょう。

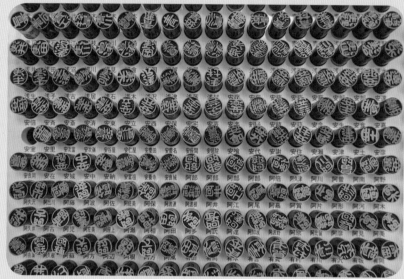

ずらりと並んだ印鑑売り場

英語で言うと？

刻印された：**carved**　朱肉：**vermilion ink pad**　書類：**documents**　宅配便：
home delivery　公文書：**official documents**　口座：**bank account**

Photo: uopicture さんによる写真 AC からの写真

What's a *hanko*?
ハンコって何ですか？

- It's a stamp carved with a personal or company name.

  個人や社名が刻印されたスタンプのことです。

- You stamp it on documents using a red ink called *shuniku*.

  朱肉という赤いインクを使って、書類などに押します。

☐ carve
　動 彫る；切り分ける
☐ personal
　形 個人の
☐ document
　名 公文書

🙂 They're usually made of wood or plastic.

その素材の多くは木やプラスチックなどです。

When do you use them?
どんな時に使いますか？

🙂 We use them instead of a signature when accepting mail and deliveries.

郵便物、宅配物の受け取りにサインの代わりとして使います。

□ instead of
　〜の代わりに
□ signature
　名 サイン
□ accept　動 受け取る
□ delivery
　名 配達 (物)

🙂 At work we stamp our *hanko* to show understanding and intent.

仕事において、了解意思表示として、ハンコを押します。

□ intent
　名 意図；合意

🙂 When correcting an official document, we draw a double line and then stamp a "correction stamp" to prove that the correction was made by the actual person.

公文書を訂正する時にも、二重線を引いてから、「訂正印」というハンコを押して、訂正したのが本人であることを証明します。

□ correct
　動 訂正する
□ correction
　名 訂正
□ prove　動 証明する
□ actual person
　実在の人物

What kinds of *hanko* are there?
どんな種類があるのですか？

🙂 The *hanko* used to open a bank account are called "ginko-in".

銀行の口座などの開設時に使うハンコは「銀行印」と呼ばれます。

□ bank account
　銀行口座

🙂 The stamp we use when receiving mail and deliveries is a "mitome-in".

郵便や宅配物を受け取るときは「認印」を使います。

🙂 At work, we often use "shachihata" stamps that don't need ink because there is ink inside them.

仕事では、インクが内蔵されていて、朱肉を使わないでも押せる「シャチハタ」がよく使われます。

扇子
Sensu (folding fan)

 40

きれいな絵柄の扇子は、お土産としてお勧めなのはもちろんですが、年々厳しくなる日本の夏の暑さ対策のためにも強くお勧めしたい一品です。

夏を涼しく演出するすだれと扇子

英語で言うと？

メモ用紙：**note paper** あおぐ：**fan oneself** 折りたたむ：**fold** （扇子の）骨：**rib (of a fan)** 持ち運びやすい **easy to carry**： 末広がり：**widen toward the end**

How long have there been "sensu"?
扇子はいつからあるの？

They first appeared in Kyoto, around the beginning of the Heian period.

平安時代の初めごろ、京都で誕生しました。

Sensu, or folding fans, began with the combination of many thin sheets used as memo paper of about 30 centimeters in length.

☐ folding fan 扇子
☐ combination
图 組み合わせ (たもの)

メモ用紙として使われていた長さ約30cm の薄い木を何枚も合わせたものが扇子の始まりです。

 Some say they assumed their present form from the Kamakura period.

☐ assume
動 〜と仮定する

今のような形になったのは、鎌倉時代からと言われています。

 Are *sensu* popular in Japan?
扇子は日本で人気があるの？

They are so popular that, in summer, stores set up areas to sell *sensu*.

夏になると、店には扇子売場ができるほど人気があります。

There are many different designs and color patterns, and almost all Japanese people own them.

さまざまなデザインや色柄のものがあり、ほとんどの日本人が持っています。

They are durable even when carried around, and some even come with cases.

持ち歩いても壊れにくい、ケースつきの扇子も人気です。

 Where do you recommend purchasing *sensu*?
扇子はどこで買うのがおすすめ？

There are various types of *sensu* available at major department stores.

有名デパートはいろいろな種類の扇子があります。

If you want an inexpensive *sensu*, I would recommend buying one at a hundred-yen shop.

安い扇子が欲しかったら100円ショップで買うのがおすすめです。

For those who want a good-quality *sensu* they can use for a long time, I would recommend buying one at a shop that specializes in *sensu*.

いいものを長く使いたい人は扇子専門店で買うのがおすすめです。

くらし・習慣

111

THEME 41

たわし
Scrub brush

「たわし」といえばこの形！と言っていいほど我々日本人におなじみの「亀の子たわし」は、1つ1つ手作りされている。お土産にピッタリ！

英語で言うと？

調理器具：**cooking equipment**　シュロ（植物）：**trachycarpus**
ホームセンター：**home improvement store**　家庭用品：**household products**
ステレス：**stainless steel**　化学繊維：**synthetic fiber**

Photo: きぬさらさんによる写真 AC からの写真

How do Japanese people use "tawashi"?
日本人はたわしをどう使ってるの？

We use them to clean cooking equipment such as cutting boards and pots.

まな板や鍋などの調理器具を洗うのに使います。

We also use them to clean vegetables such as potatoes and carrots.

じゃがいもや人参など野菜洗いにも使います。

☐ scrub brush
たわし

☐ cooking equipment
調理器具

🙂 There are also some people who use softer *tawashi* to clean their bodies.

やわらかめのたわしで体を洗う人もいます。

Where do you recommend purchasing *tawashi*?

たわしはどこで買うのがおすすめ？

🙂 You can find them in the household products section at department stores, supermarkets, and home improvement stores.

デパートやスーパー、ホームセンターの家庭用品売り場にあります。

☐ household product 家庭用品
☐ home improvement store 日曜大工店

🙂 There are also *tawashi* manufacturers who sell limited edition models either through online shops or chain stores.

オンラインショップや直営店だけで買える限定品を出しているたわしメーカーもあります。

🙂 You can experience making *tawashi* at a store directly managed by a *tawashi* manufacturer.

たわしメーカーの直営店なら、たわし作り体験ができます

☐ manufacturer
名 製造業者

How long have there been *tawashi*?

たわしはいつからあるの？

🙂 *Tawashi* first appeared in Tokyo about 100 years ago.

たわしは今から約100年前に東京で生まれました。

🙂 *Tawashi* have been the same shape for almost 100 years.

たわしは約100年前からずっと同じ形です。

🙂 These days, *tawashi* made from stainless steel or synthetic fiber are also being sold.

最近は、ステンレスや化学繊維で作られたものも売っています。

☐ synthetic fiber
合成繊維

桐たんす
Paulownia Chest

THEME
42

🔽 42

高級家具の代名詞である桐のたんす。その理由や機能性はもとより、現代の生活スタイルに合わせた新製品などについてもご案内してみましょう。

英語で言うと？

湿度：**humidity**　害虫：**insects**；**pest**　燃えにくい：**fire-resistant**
修理する：**repair**　取っ手：**handle**　嫁入り道具：**trousseau**

Photo: naon さんによる写真 AC からの写真

What's good about a paulownia chest?
桐たんすのいいところは？

Paulownia adjusts its temperature to ward off insects, enabling clothing to be kept in a good state.

桐は湿度を調整して害虫を寄せ付けないため、衣類をいい状態で保管できます。

☐ paulownia 名 桐

☐ ward off 避ける
☐ enable
　動 〜を可能にする

114

Paulownia is fire-resistant and does not burn easily, so even if a fire does occur, clothing is kept safe.

桐は火に強く燃えにくいため、万が一火事が起こっても衣類を安全に守ります。

☐ fire-resistant
形 耐火性の

Paulownia chests can be repaired, so they can be used for a long time.

桐たんすは修理ができるので、長く使うことができます。

☐ repair
動 ～を修理する

How long have paulownia chests been around?

桐たんすはいつからあるの？

They first appeared in Osaka, and began to be used from the Edo period through the beginning of the Meiji period.

大阪で誕生し、江戸時代から明治時代初めごろにかけて使うようになりました。

▶ かつては女の子が生まれると庭に桐を植えて、嫁入りの際にそれでたんすを作って持たせたそうです

Houses during this period did not have rooms, and the chests had handles and were light so they could be carried when necessary.

この時代の家には部屋がなかったので、必要なときに持ち運べるように取っ手つきで軽いものでした。

There was a custom where the chest was given as trousseau when a woman got married.

女の子が結婚するときに、嫁入り道具として持たせる習慣もありました。

☐ trousseau
名 嫁入り衣装

Recently, cool-looking chests and smaller chests have emerged, and are attracting the attention of young people.

最近はおしゃれなものや小ぶりのたんすなども登場して、若い人たちが注目しています。

☐ cool-looking
かっこいい
☐ emerge
動 現れる；わかってくる

THEME 43
はたき
Duster

43

かつて一般的だった布製のものから、化学繊維や静電気を使った使い捨てモップで高いところのホコリをとることが今では主流になっていますね。

英語で言うと？

化学繊維：**synthetic fiber** 静電気：**static electricity** 精密機械：**precision machine** 鳥の羽：**feather** 使い捨て：**disposable** 高級旅館：**luxury inn**

Photo: ななほしてんとうさんによる写真 AC からの写真

What types of "hataki," or dusters, are there?

はたきにはどんな種類があるの？

Since the Edo period, there have been *hataki* with cloth on a handle, making it easy to clean high or narrow places.

江戸時代からあるのは布が柄についたはたきで、高い所や狭い所も掃除しやすいです。

□ paulownia 名 桐

□ ward off 避ける
□ enable
　　動 ～を可能にする

- *Hataki* with synthetic fiber in the cloth can capture dust using static electricity, so it's perfect for cleaning precision machines like computers.

  化学繊維が柄についたはたきは、静電気でほこりがとれるので、パソコンなどの精密機械の掃除にぴったりです。

☐ static electricity
静電気
☐ precision machine
精密機械

- *Hataki* with feathers on the cloth are soft, making it easy to collect fine dust particles.

  鳥の羽などが柄についたはたきは、やわらかいので、細かなほこりがとりやすいです。

☐ particle 名 粒子

How do you clean with *hataki*?
はたきでどうやって掃除するの？

- Open the windows, tap on high shelves and other such things, and let the dust fall to the floor.

  窓を開け、高い棚などにたまったほこりをたたいて床に落とします。

- Clean up the dust that has fallen to the floor with a rag or vacuum cleaner.

  床に落ちたほこりは、ほうきや掃除機できれいにします。

- In the past, people would cover their head with a towel to avoid getting dust on themselves.

  昔は、自分にほこりがかからないように、頭にてぬぐいをかぶって掃除していました。

- These days, most households clean up dust using disposable mops.

  最近は、使い捨てモップでほこりをとる家庭がほとんどです。

☐ disposable
形 使い捨てできる

- It seems that luxury "ryokan," or inns, with Japanese rooms, as well as Japanese restaurants, still clean with *hataki*.

  和室のある高級旅館や日本料理店などは、今もはたきで掃除しているようです。

☐ luxury 形 高級な

ほうき
Houki (broom)

 44

ほうきは一般的な生活用具ですが、伝統的な和帚の中には何十年も使える高品質のものもあります。場所もとらないし音も静か、何よりエコ！

英語で言うと？
- -

室内：**indoor**　屋外：**outdoor**　シュロ（植物）：**palm tree**　（箒の）柄：**handle (of a broom)**　神事：**religious services**　玄関：**entryway of home**

Photo: キャプテンフック / PIXTA (ピクスタ)

Is it common in Japan to clean using "houki"?
日本はほうきで掃除するのが普通なの？

While in many cases *houki*, or brooms, are used to clean in classrooms and outdoors at schools, primarily vaccum cleaners are used to clean homes.

学校の教室や屋外はほうきで掃除することが多いですが、家の掃除はほとんど掃除機を使います。

□ in many cases
　多くの場合
□ broom　名 ほうき
□ primarily
　副 主に；当初は

118

- Before vacuum cleaners spread, we used to use *houki* to clean.

  掃除機が普及する前は、家の掃除もほうきを使っていました。

- Long ago, laying wet tea leaves in rooms of "tatami," or straw mats, and cleaning them with *houki* was popular because they could capture most of the dirt.

  昔は、濡れた茶葉をたたみの部屋にまいてほうきで掃除すると、ごみがよく取れて人気でした。

□ lay
　動 ～を置く；横たえる
□ capture
　動 ～をとらえる

What types of *houki* are there?
ほうきはどんな種類があるの？

- There is a *houki* with a long handle for use outdoors to clean things like fallen leaves.

  落ち葉などを掃除する、柄の長い屋外用のほうきがあります。

- There is also a *houki* with a short handle for use indoors to clean tatami rooms and other areas.

  たたみの部屋などを掃除する、柄の短い室内用のほうきがあります。

- And there is a palm-sized *houki* for use in cleaning desktops and such areas.

  机の上などを掃除する、手のひらサイズのほうきもあります。

□ palm-sized　手のひらサイズの
□ desktop
　名 机の上

How long has Japan had *houki*?
日本にはいつからほうきがあるの？

- It is said we have had it since the Kofun period, but apparently it was not used as a cleaning tool.

  古墳時代からあると言われていますが、掃除道具としては使っていなかったようです。

□ apparently
　副 どうも～らしい

⏺ Since the Nara period, the *houki* became a tool used at festivals for deities, and was to be treated with great respect.

奈良時代以降、ほうきは神様の祭りで使う道具となって大切に扱わなくてはいけないものとなりました。

⏺ Japanese legend has it that if you stand the broom in your home's entryway with the broomstick pointed downward, it is tantamount to saying to uninvited guests or to those who have overstayed their welcome, "please leave."

日本の言い伝えで、ほうきの柄を下にして玄関に立てかけるのは、お客さんに「帰ってください」言っているのに等しい行為です。

□ deity　名 神

□ entryway　名 通路
□ broomstick
　名 ほうきの柄
□ point
　動 ～を向ける；指す
□ downward
　副 下に
□ tantamount
　形 ～に等しい

学校の教室や廊下、トイレなどを生徒が掃除することは、日本ではごく当たり前の光景。ですが、国によっては非常に驚かれることも。

Photo: Fast&Slow / PIXTA (ピクスタ)

120

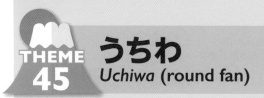

うちわ
Uchiwa (round fan)

 45

近年では本来の使い方である「あおぐ」以外にも、推しを応援したり広告宣伝用に配ったりと、いろいろな場面で使われていますね！

英語で言うと？

顔を隠す：**hide one's own face**　害虫：**pest**　広告の道具：**as advertising tool**
高級な：**high quality**　観賞用：**ornamental**　布：**fabric**

Photo: Fast&Slow / PIXTA (ピクスタ)

How long have "uchiwa" been around? How are they different from *sensu*?

うちわはいつからあるの？　扇子と何が違うの？

They came from China in the Kofun period, and the handle was longer then than it is now. *Sensu* is the result of making the *uchiwa*, or round fan, portable and easy to carry.

□ result
　名 結果；効果
□ portable
　形 携帯用の

くらし・習慣

古墳時代に中国から伝えられ、今よりも柄が長めでした。うちわを携帯しやすいように折り畳みにしたのが扇子です。

It was a tool used by people of high social status to hide their own faces or to shoo away pests.

偉い人物が自分の顔を隠したり、害虫を払いよける道具として使っていました。

- [ ] social status
  社会的地位
- [ ] shoo away
  シッシッと追い払う
- [ ] pest 名 害虫

It is said that they began to be used in daily life such as to cool oneself by fanning or to start a fire from around the Edo period.

扇いで涼んだり火を起こすなど生活で使うようになったのは江戸時代ごろからと言われています。

- [ ] fan
  動 ～に風を送る

Are there uses for *uchiwa* other than fanning to cool oneself?

扇いで涼む以外に使い方はあるの？

There are also many people who use them as goods to cheer on pop stars and celebrities.

アイドルやタレントなどを応援するグッズとして使う人も多いです。

- [ ] cheer on
  声援する
- [ ] pop star
  ポップ・スター

Some companies use them as advertising tools, distributing them for free to many people.

企業が広告の道具として使い、たくさんの人に無料で配ることがあります。

- [ ] advertising tool
  広告宣伝ツール
- [ ] distribute
  動 ～を分配する

Young people use them as fashion items when taking part in festivals.

祭に参加するときのファッションとして若者が使います。

What types of *uchiwa* are there?
うちわにはどんな種類がある？

Most *uchiwa* that are made of bamboo and Japanese paper are of high quality, and some are strictly ornamental.

竹と和紙でできているうちわは高級なものが多く、鑑賞用のものもあります。

Most *uchiwa* that are made of plastic and paper can be purchased at reasonable prices, and some are distributed at no charge.

プラスチックと紙でできているうちわは安く買えるものが多く、無料で配っているものもあります。

There are also *uchiwa* where you can create your own design, and those made of fabric that can be folded very small.

好きなデザインにできるうちわや、布製で小さく畳めるうちわもあります。

□ strictly
副 厳密に；完全に
□ ornamental
形 装飾用の

□ reasonable
形 合理的な；さほど高くない

くらし・習慣

Photo: sunabesyou / PIXTA (ピクスタ)

てぬぐい
Towel

 46

最近では様々な絵柄のものも増えて、選ぶ楽しみが増えているてぬぐい。っ
特に夏場は、外で振り回していれば、濡れていてもすぐに乾いて便利！

英語で言うと？

仏像：**Buddha statue** 　高級品：**luxury item** 　庶民：**common people**
糸の織り方：**weaving technique** 　肌触り：**feel** 　吸水性：**absorben**

Photo: kai / PIXTA (ピクスタ)

How long have there been "tenugui", or towels, in Japan?

日本のてぬぐいはいつからあるの？

They have been used to clean Buddha statues since the Nara period, and the material then was silk.

仏像などを掃除する布として奈良時代から使われ、素材は絹でした。

Until the Heian period, it was a luxury item that only people of high social standing could use.

平安時代までは、身分の高い人しか使えない高級品でした。

It also spread to common people from around the Kamakura period, and became the cotton material of today from the Edo period.

鎌倉時代のころから庶民にも広がり、今のような綿素材になったのは江戸時代からです。

What's the difference between *tenugui* and a regular towel?

てぬぐいとタオルの違いは？

Both are made from cotton material, but the weaving technique is different, so the thickness and feel are different.

どちらも綿素材ですが、糸の織り方が違うので、肌触りや厚みが違います。

Towels are more absorbent than *tenugui*.

てぬぐいよりもタオルのほうが吸水性が高いです。

Compared to towels, *tenugui* are easy to dry and can be folded very small.

てぬぐいはタオルに比べて乾きやすく小さくたためます。

How do you recommend using *tenugui*?

おすすめのてぬぐいの使い方は？

You can wear it on your head like a hat, or wrap it around your neck and make it a cool fashion item.

帽子のように頭にかぶったり、首に巻くとおしゃれグッズとして使えます。

くらし・習慣

It's also fun to use it as a case for plastic bottles, or to wrap presents.

ペットボトルケースにしたり、プレゼントのラッピングに使っても楽しいです。

☐ plastic bottle
ペットボトル

It looks very nice as a wall hanging as part of interior room decoration.

部屋のインテリアとして壁に飾ってもステキです。

☐ wall hanging
壁掛け

Photo: Fast&Slow / PIXTA (ピクスタ)

126

THEME 47
のれん
Shop Curtain

 47

のれんの目的や種類について、かんたんに説明してみましょう。ちなみに
玄関先に長いのれんをかけると、省エネにつながりおすすめです！

英語で言うと？

塵：**dust**　隠す：**hide**　絵柄：**pattern**　看板：**sign**　ディスプレー：**display**
仕切り：**divider**

Photo: bamuse / PIXTA（ピクスタ）

くらし・習慣

How long have there been "noren", or shop curtains, in Japan?

日本ののれんはいつからあるの？

According to historical records, they were
used at the homes of common people in
the Heian period.

史料によると、平安時代の庶民の家で使われていたとされてい
ます。

☐ historical record
歴史的記録物

127

💬 They were used to protect homes from sunlight, cold, wind, and dust, and to hide the inside of the home.

のれんは日差しや寒さ、風・塵（ちり）から家を守り、部屋の様子を隠すために使われていました。

💬 They began to have characters or patterns on them from the Kamakura period.

鎌倉時代からは文字や絵柄などが描かれるようになりました。

How are *noren* used around town?
街中ではどんなふうにのれんを使っているの？

💬 They are used as signs, sunshades, displays, and eye-catching dividers.

看板、日よけ、ディスプレー、人目をよける仕切りなどに使われています。

☐ sunshade
　名 日よけ
☐ display
　名 表示；陳列
☐ eye-catching
　人目をひく
☐ divider　名 仕切り

💬 At some shops, displaying *noren* indicates that the shop is open, and if the *noren* is not out, it means that the shop is closed.

一部の店では、のれんが出ていると開店中を示し、出ていないと閉店したことを知らせます。

☐ indicate
　動 ～ということを示す

💬 When someone who had worked at a shop quits to set up their own shop, we call that "noren wake," where the shop owner helps them establish their business.

店に勤めていた人が辞めて自分の店を出すことを「のれん分け」と言います。

☐ establish
　動 設立する

What types of *noren* are there?

のれんには種類があるの？

● The most common is the one that is about 113 centimeters in length. But there are also "han noren" which are about 56.7 centimeters, "naga noren," which are about 160 centimeters, and "mizuhiki noren," which are about 40 centimeters.

長さ約113cm が一般的なサイズです。約56.7cm の「半のれん」、約160cm の「長のれん」、約40cm の「水引のれん」などもあります。

● There are "gakuya noren," which people such as *kabuki* actors hang in the dressing room, and "yu noren," used at bathing facilities to indicate whether a bathroom is for women or men.

歌舞伎役者などが楽屋につるす「楽屋のれん」、入浴施設で男女の浴室を示す「湯のれん」があります。

□ dressing room
楽屋

● In the Hokuriku region, when a daughter is to be married, that family gives a "hanayome noren" that bears the family mark to the groom-to-be's family as a present.

北陸地方では娘が結婚するとき、結婚相手の家に「花嫁のれん」という家のマークが入ったのれんを贈ります。

□ region　名 地域
□ bear
　動 持つ；有する
□ groom-to-be
　婚約している男性

くらし・習慣

THEME 48

うるし
Lacquer

48

お手頃価格で購入できる、普段使いのお椀などから美しく高級な品物まで、漆器は人気の工芸品です。全国30以上の都府県で生産されています。

英語で言うと？

土器：**earthenware**　木製品：**wooden product**　遺跡：**ruin**　刀の鞘：**sword sheath**　宝物：**treasure**　長所：**benefit**　樹液：**sap**　酸：**acid**　アルカリ：**alkali**　防水：**water-proof**　防虫：**insect-proof**　抗菌：**anti-bacteria**　つやのある：**glossy**

Photo: omizu / PIXTA (ピクスタ)

How long has there been "urushi," or lacquer, in Japan?

日本のうるしはいつからあるの？

It was learned through excavations of ruins that it was used during the Jomon period to repair earthenware, and applied to wooden products.

縄文時代の土器の補修に使ったり、木製品に塗って使っていたことが遺跡調査からわかっています。

☐ excavation
　名 掘削（した穴）
☐ ruin　名 遺跡；荒廃
☐ earthenware
　名 土器

When the Nara period came, it was applied to a sword sheath, which is preserved as a treasure at the Shosoin Repository at Todaiji Temple.

奈良時代になると、刀の鞘（さや／刀の入れ物）に塗られ、東大寺の正倉院に宝物として保管されています。

Once the Edo period came around, lacquered products began to be developed, primarily in the northern part of the country.

江戸時代に入ると、主に北国で漆塗り製品が開発されるようになりました。

□ sword sheath
刀の鞘

□ preserve
動 保存する

□ repository
名 保存場所；博物館

What are the benefits of products that use *urushi*?

うるしを使った製品の長所は？

Sap is the raw material, which makes it safe for people and the environment.

原料が樹液で、人にも環境にもやさしいことです。

It is resistant to acid and alkali, in addition to being water- and insect-proof and having anti-bacterial effects, so it is not easily damaged and lasts for a long time.

酸やアルカリに強く、防水・防虫・抗菌効果もあるので、傷みにくく長く使えます。

The more you use it, the glossier it becomes, increasing the merits of *urushi*.

使えば使うほどつやが出て、うるしのよさが増してきます。

□ benefit 名 長所

□ sap 名 樹液

□ raw material
原料

□ resistant
形 耐久性 [抵抗力] のある

□ acid 名 酸

□ alkali 名 アルカリ

□ anti-bacterial
形 抗菌性のある

□ effect 名 効果

□ glossy
形 光沢のある

□ merit
名 長所；利点

くらし・習慣

What products using *urushi* do you recommend?

うるしを使ったおすすめ商品は？

□ tableware
名 食卓用食器類

I recommend regularly used tableware such as plates and bowls.

普段の食事でよく使う皿やお椀などの食器はおすすめです。

Products other than tableware, such as pens, smartphone cases, and mirrors also look cool.

ペンやスマホケース、鏡など、食器以外の商品もおしゃれです。

You can also choose an interior item such as a photo stand or vase, and that would look nice.

インテリアの1つに写真立てや花瓶などを選んでもステキです。

石川県輪島漆芸美術館
常時全室で漆芸品を展示している、世界で唯一の美術館（もちろん石川県輪島市にある）。日本が世界に誇る優れた漆文化の発信拠点として、1991（平成3）年に開館。四季折々の企画展に加え、常設展では輪島塗の歴史と文化を展示している

写真提供：石川県観光連盟

THEME 49

日傘
Parasol

 49

年々暑さも紫外線も強烈になる日本の夏の必須アイテム＝日傘。これまでは、女性が使うイメージでしたが、男性用の商品も増えています。

くらし・習慣

英語で言うと？

紫外線：**ultraviolet ray**　強くなる：**become strong**　日焼け防止：**prevent sunburn**　熱中症：**sunstroke**　長傘：**long-ribbed parasol**　折りたためる：**collapsible**

Photo: On and On / PIXTA (ピクスタ)

Are parasols attracting attention in Japan?
日本では日傘が注目されているのですか？

Parasols are most useful in Japan from around May, when ultraviolet rays become strong.

紫外線が強くなる5月ごろから、日本では日傘が活躍します。

□ ultraviolet ray
紫外線

133

🌀 Recently, parasols for men are also popular.

最近は、男性用の日傘も人気です。

🌀 The fact that the Ministry of the Environment recommends them not only to prevent sunburn, but also as a protective measure against sunstroke.

環境省が、日焼け防止だけでなく熱中症対策としても奨（すす）めていることも理由かもしれません。

☐ Ministry of the Environment
環境省

☐ sunburn　名 日焼け

☐ protective measures
安全対策

☐ sunstroke
名 日射病

What kinds of parasols are there?
どのような種類がありますか？

🌀 In addition to the usual long-ribbed parasol, there are parasols that are collapsible, lightweight, and those with functions such as complete protection from light.

通常の長傘のほか、折りたたみ、軽量、完全遮光などいろんな機能を持った日傘があります。

☐ ribbed
形 うねのある

☐ collapsible
形 折りたたみできる

☐ lightweight
形 軽量の

🌀 In addition to general parasols made from cotton or hemp, there are those usable in both nice or rainy weather.

綿や麻でできた一般的な日傘のほか、晴雨兼用のものもあります。

☐ usable
形 使い物になる

🌀 Today there are also superlight-weight parasols on the 100-gram level, so they are very convenient to carry.

最近では100グラム台の超軽量日傘もあるので、持ち運びに便利です。

☐ superlight
形 超軽量の

Since when have parasols been used in Japan?

日本ではいつごろから傘を使っているのですか？

Just like Buddhism, green tea and *kanji* characters, it is said that parasols were introduced by China around the Heian Era.

平安時代前後に仏教やお茶・漢字等と同じく中国より伝来したと言われています。

At the time, they were using ancient Japanese umbrellas and Japanese umbrellas made using bamboo and Japanese paper.

当時は、竹と和紙で作られた日本古来の傘・和傘を使っていました。

☐ ancient
形 古代の;時代がかった

It is said that we began to be able to open and close umbrellas like today during the Azuchi-Momoyama period.

現在のように傘が開閉できるようになったのは安土桃山時代と言われています。

Photo: m.Taira / PIXTA (ピクスタ)

内祝い
Uchiiwai

 50

日本人でもあまりピンとこない人もいるかもしれません。この機会にお作法を覚えて、きちんと説明できるようになりましょう。

英語で言うと？ ----------------------------------

出産：**childbirth**　新築：**building a new house**　記念の：**commemorative**
親族：**relative**　目上の人：**superior**　マナー違反：**bad manners**

What is an *uchiiwai*?
内祝いってなんですか？

It's when there is a celebration among your inner circle such as marriage, childbirth or building a new house, and you give commemorative gifts.

結婚、出産、新築など内輪のお祝い事があったときに、記念になる品物を贈ることです。

□ celebration
　名 お祝い
□ inner circle
　小集団
□ commemorative
　形 記念の

136

● The gifts are sent to show thanks for the people who help you and the people who care about you.

お世話になっている人や、気にかけてくれている人たちに感謝の気持ちを込めて送ります。

□ care about
　〜を大切にする

● Nowadays it also refers to thanks given for those celebrations.

現在では、それらのお祝いをもらった時のお礼のことも指すようになりました。

□ nowadays
　副 最近は
□ refer to
　〜に言及する；〜を参照する

How much money do people give in return?
お返しの金額はどれくらいかかるのですか？

● Basically, it's called "han-gaeshi", and you send back about half of the amount you get.

基本的には半返しと呼ばれ、もらった額の半額程度を送ります。

□ amount　名 量；額

● If the giver is a relative or superior, you might give one-third back.

親族や目上の人であれば1／3程度を返すこともあります。

□ giver　名 贈与者
□ relative
　名 血縁者；身内
□ superior
　形 目上の；優れた
　名 上司

● Sending something more expensive than the person gave you is bad manners.

相手からの頂き物より高いものを送るのはマナー違反です。

What are the rules?
どんな決まりがあるのですか？

● For private birthday celebrations, you attach a decoration with the person's name on it to unveil their name.

出産の内祝いの場合、名前をお披露目する意味を込めて、贈り物には名前の入ったのしをつけます。

□ attach　動 添える
□ decoration
　名 装飾
□ unveil　動 明かす

● You return the gifts about one month after giving birth or getting married.

出産後、挙式後の1ヶ月前後を目安にお返しをします。

137

田舎暮らし
Country Life

🔽 51

田舎暮らしを好む欧米の人たちはたくさんいますので、「日本の田舎暮らし事情」がどうなっているのか、興味津々です！

英語で言うと？

長期休暇：**extended vacation**　退職する：**quit one's job**　定年退職する：**retire**
老夫婦：**elderly couple**　農作物：**crops**　農作業：**farming**

Photo: sasaki106 / PIXTA (ピクスタ)

How do Japanese people approach country life?
日本人はどんなふうに田舎暮らしをするの？

😊 There are many people who experience country life just during extended vacations.

長期休暇の期間だけ、田舎暮らしを体験する人は多いです。

😊 There are also people who quit their jobs and move to a place where they can live the country life.

仕事を辞めて田舎暮らしをする場所に引っ越す人もいます。

□ quit 動 辞める

138

😊 And there are people who live the country life only on weekends.

週末だけ、田舎暮らしをする人もいます。

What kinds of people like country life?
田舎暮らしはどんな人に人気？

😊 It is popular among families with young children.

小さな子どもがいる家族に人気があります。

😊 There are also many retired elderly couples.

定年退職した老夫婦も多いです。

☐ retired
形 引退した

😊 And it is popular among men and women in their thirties and forties.

30〜40代の男性や女性にも人気があります。

Why is country life popular?
田舎暮らしはどうして人気があるの？

😊 Because people can live a healthy life with no stress raising crops in an environment rich in nature.

自然豊かな環境で、農作物を育てるなどストレスのない健康的な生活が送れるからです。

☐ raise crops
作物を育てる

😊 Because moving to a place where we can enjoy country life makes us eligible to potentially receive subsidies for rent and moving expenses.

田舎暮らしをする場所に移住すると、家賃や引越し代などを出してくれることがあるからです。

☐ eligible
形 適格な；ふさわしい
☐ potentially
副 潜在的に
☐ subsidy
名 助成金；交付金
☐ expense
名 費用；経費

😊 Because, depending on where we move to, there is support such as introductions to work and free education for children.

移住先によっては、仕事を紹介してくれたり、子どもの塾の費用が無料になるなどのサポートがあるからです。

☐ support
名 支援；援助
☐ introduction
名 紹介

忘年会
Bonenkai

52

勤め先、取引先、ママ友、学友、旧友…などなど、さまざまな忘年会がありますが、ここでは会社で行われる忘年会をテーマに解説します。

英語で言うと？ -

混む：**become crowded**　路線：**route**　増便する：**add trains**
取引先：**business partner**　上司：**superior**　つぎ足す：**refill**

Photo: satoko / PIXTA (ピクスタ)

When are *bonenkai* held?
忘年会っていつ行われるの？

🎎 The name means "forgetting the year",
so they're held at the end of the year.

その年を忘れるという意味合いがあるので、年末に行われます。

🎎 Companies that you often do business
with hold *bonenkai* from around the end
of November.

付合いの多い会社などは11月末頃から忘年会が行われ始めます。

🙂 The last trains on those days are terribly crowded, so depending on the line they may add trains.

その時期の終電は大変混み合うので、路線によっては増便されることがあります。

What is a *bonenkai*?

忘年会ってなに？

🙂 It's a party you hold at work or with friends to thank people for their hard work during the year.

その年の労をねぎらって、会社や友人間で行われる会です。

🙂 They're mostly held in workplaces and between friends. At workplaces, there might be many held for different departments and different business partners.

主に会社や友人間で行われます。会社では、部署別、取引先別などで何度も行われたりします。

🙂 Some of them also go on for a long time, with one or two afterparties.

２次会、３次会など長時間に渡って行われることもあります。

Is there etiquette for banquets?

宴会でのマナーはあるの？

🙂 Generally you pour *sake* for your superiors and business partners.

基本的に上司や取引先の人にお酒を注ぎます。

🙂 They might want to order a different drink next, so ask before you refill their drink.

次は違う飲み物を頼みたいこともあるので、つぎ足してもいいかを確認しましょう。

🙂 When someone fills a drink for you, gently place your hand on the bottom of the glass.

お酒を注いでもらうときには、グラスの底に手を軽く当てます。

□ terribly　副 ひどく
□ depending on
　〜次第で

□ workplace
　名 仕事場
□ department
　名 部署

□ afterparty
　二次会

□ banquet
　名 宴会；ごちそう

□ pour　動 注ぐ

□ refill
　動 〜を補充する

□ fill　動 満たす
□ gently
　副 静かに；優しく

141

THEME 53 新年会
Shinnenkai

↓ 53

「お年玉」や昔ながらの遊びなど、お正月にまつわるトピックについてや、会社で行われる新年会の内容や目的も説明してみましょう。

英語で言うと？

親族：**family; relative**　お小遣い：**allowance**　かるた：**traditional Japanese playing cards**　福笑い：**Japanese version of pin the tail on the donkey**
偉い人：**higher-up**　従業員：**employee**

Photo: ゲタゲタさんによる写真 AC からの写真

What's a *shinnenkai*?
新年会って何？

A *shinnenkai* is a party you hold with people close to you at the beginning of a new year.

新年会とは、新しい年の幕開けを祝って親しい人と行う宴です。

☐ at the beginning of　〜の初めに

At companies, it also means that you wish for the success of the company in the new year.

会社では、その年の会社の発展を祈願する意味合いもあります。

🙂 Sometimes they are also held with the employees of another company that you do business with.

また、付き合いのある他の会社の人たちと行うこともあります。

What do you do at *shinnenkai*?
新年会では何をするの？

🙂 You get together with your family and drink *sake*, and eat a New Year's meal called "osechi".

親族などで集まってお酒を飲んだり、「おせち」と呼ばれるお正月の料理を食べたりします。

🙂 Adults give children an allowance called "otoshidama".

大人は子供に「お年玉」と呼ばれるお小遣いをあげたりします。

🙂 Sometimes people play old-fashioned games like *karuta*, *hyakunin-isshu* or *fukuwarai*.

かるたや百人一首、福笑いなど昔ながらの遊びをすることもあります。

What do you do at company New Year's parties?
会社の新年会ではどんなことをするの？

🙂 The higher-ups announce the policies and goals for the new year.

偉い人がその年の経営方針や目標などを発表します。

🙂 After the greetings, everyone says cheers and drinks *sake* and other drinks.

挨拶の後に全員で乾杯をして、お酒などを飲みます。

🙂 It also has the purpose of getting people out of holiday-mode and ready to work again.

お正月休み気分を引き締めて、仕事や生活を新たな気持ちで始めましょうという意味合いもあります。

くらし・習慣

THEME 54 レストランの無料の水
Free Water at Restaurants

 54

日本ではほとんどの飲食店で「お冷や」として水が無料で供されますが、
これは外国の方々から見ると、必ずしも当たり前のことではありません。

英語で言うと？

飲料水：**potable water**　水道：**water pipe**　サービスとして：**as a service**
雨水：**rainwater**　設備：**facility**　公共施設：**public facility**

Photo: Betty（ベティ）さんによる写真 AC からの写真

Why is water served at no charge at restaurants?
レストランで無料の水が出てくるのはなぜ？

💬 Because water from the water supply in Japan is safe to drink.

日本は安全に飲める水が水道から出るからです。

💬 In Japan, there is a culture known as "omotenashi," or hospitality, and water is provided as a service in that spirit.

□ hospitality
名 もてなし

144

日本には「おもてなし」の文化があり、サービスとして出しています。

🗣 Because there are facilities in Japan for collecting rainwater, so water is abundant.

日本は雨水を溜める設備が整っていて水が豊富にあるからです。

☐ abundant
形 豊富な

Besides restaurants, at what other kinds of places can you drink water for free?
レストラン以外で水が無料で飲めるのはどんな場所？

🗣 We can drink it at public facilities such as city offices, libraries, and parks.

市役所、図書館、公園などの公共施設で飲めます。

🗣 We can also drink it at supermarkets, department stores, and hospitals.

スーパーマーケット、デパートや病院でも飲めます。

🗣 We can even drink it at several subway stations.

東京のいくつかの地下鉄駅でも飲めます。

Besides water, do restaurants offer anything else at no charge?
レストランで水以外に無料で提供しているものはあるの？

🗣 There are some restaurants that serve tea for free.

お茶が出てくるレストランもあります。

🗣 There are restaurants that offer damp washcloths.

おしぼりが出てくるレストランもあります。

☐ damp 形 湿った
☐ washcloth
名 手ぬぐい

☐ portion
名 一人前 (の量)

🗣 And there are restaurants that offer additional portions of rice or *miso* soup for free.

ごはんやみそ汁がおかわり自由なレストランもあります。

長い行列
Long Lines

 55

人気店や限定品、福袋、テーマパークのアトラクションや美術館など、さまざまなところで長〜い行列ができる、不思議の国、ニッポン！

英語で言うと？

福袋：**lucky bag**　飲食店：**restaurant**　じっと待つ：**wait patiently**
教育：**education**　幼少期：**early childhood**　慣れている：**be used to**

Photo: fuku41さんによる写真 AC からの写真

Why do restaurants have long lines in front of them?

レストランに長い行列ができるのはなぜ？

🔘 Because we see them introduced on television or through social media, and want to go.

テレビ番組やSNSでレストランの紹介を見て行きたくなるからです。

Because from a very young age, we are taught to wait patiently in line for a long time. We are used to lines.

長時間並んだりじっと待つ教育を幼少期から受けていて、行列に慣れているからです。

Because we assume that a restaurant with a long line in front of it serves more delicious food than a restaurant with few customers.

お客さんが少ない店よりも行列店のほうがおいしいだろうと思うからです。

□ patiently
副 根気よく

What other kinds of places have long lines in front of them?

長い行列はほかにどんな場所でできる？

Long lines form beginning on the day before a new smartphone or electrical appliance is released.

新しいスマホや家電が発売される日は、その前日から長い行列ができます。

□ electrical appliance
電気器具 [製品]

Long lines also form in front of popular attractions at amusement parks.

アミューズメントパークで人気のアトラクションも長い行列ができます。

There are long lines in front of department stores during New Year's as they sell "fukubukuro", or lucky bags.

お正月は福袋を買うために、デパートは開店前から長い行列ができます。

Some people play games or exchange information using their smartphones.

スマホでゲームや情報交換などをしている人もいます。

Other people listen to music or read.

音楽を聴いたり、読書などをしている人もいます。

THEME 56

電線の多さ
Overwhelming Number of Power Lines

 56

日本のように電柱と電線が張り巡らされている状態は、実は先進国の中では非常に珍しいことなのです。背景や理由を英語で言ってみましょう。

英語で言うと？

電線：**power line**　電柱：**utility pole**　地中：**underground**　埋める：**bury**
国道：**national road**

Photo: しみるけいさんによる写真 AC からの写真

Why are there so many power lines and utility poles in cities?

電線と電柱が街にたくさんあるのはなぜ？

Power lines first appeared in Japan in the Edo period, and as no accidents occurred, they were believed to be safe.

日本の電線は江戸時代に登場しましたが、事故が起こらなかったため、安全なものと考えられていました。

□ utility pole　電柱

After the Pacific War, Japan produced many utility poles and power lines, and they were to be buried underground in the future.

太平洋戦争後、日本は電柱と電線をたくさんつくりましたが、将来的に電線は地中に埋める予定でした。

However, the funds to bury power lines underground were not available, and as a great volume of electricity was needed immediately, the power lines stayed as they were.

ところが、電線を地中に埋めるお金がなく、すぐに多くの電気が必要だったので、電線はそのままになりました。

□ fund 名 蓄え；資金

□ electricity 名 電気；電力

Does Japan not plan to bury its power lines underground?
日本は電線を地中に埋める気がないの？

After the high economic growth period, there was a plan to bury power lines underground.

高度経済成長期のあと、電線を地中に埋める計画はありました。

□ high economic growth period 高度経済成長期

Activity to bury power lines on national roads underground is proceeding.

国道の電線は地中に埋める活動が進んでいます。

□ national road 国道
□ proceed 動 始める；続行する

Led by the Ministry of Land, Infrastructure, Transport and Tourism, activity to bury power lines underground is proceeding nationwide.

国土交通省が中心となり、全国的に電線を地中に埋める活動が進んでいます。

□ Ministry of Land, Infrastructure, Transport and Tourism 国土交通省

THEME 57 エスカレーターでの片側立ち
Standing to One Side on the Escalator

エスカレーターの利用にまつわる不思議なマナー（ルール）について、東西の違いや現状を交えて英語でご説明してみましょう！

Photo: bee / PIXTA (ピクスタ)

英語で言うと？

諸説：**various theories** 大阪万博：**Osaka World Expo** 欧米諸国：**Western countries** 追い抜く：**pass** 禁止する：**prohibit** 前提：**premise**

Are there rules for public places?
公共の場でのルールはありますか？

● When riding on an escalator, we stand in a row and leave one side open.

エスカレーターに乗る場合は、1列になって片側を空けます。

☐ stand in a row
　1列に並んで立つ

● The side that is left open differs between the Kansai and Kanto regions.

関西と関東で空ける側が違います。

In Tokyo, they stand on the left, and in Osaka, they stand on the right.

東京では左側に立ち、大阪では右側に立ちます。

Why are there different rules in the same country?

なぜ同じ国内でもルールが違うのですか？

There are various theories as to why the rules are different in Kanto and Kansai.

関東と関西でルールが異なる理由には諸説あります。

During the Osaka World Expo in 1970, it is said that Kansai learned from Western countries and left the left side open.

大阪万博（1970年）の際、関西では欧米諸国にならい、左側を空けるようにしたと言われています。

There is a theory that, in the Kanto region, just as cars drive on the left and pass on the right, they leave the right side open.

関東では車の左側通行と同じく、右から追い抜くという考えで右を空ける、という説もあります。

Has it recently become prohibited to walk on escalators?

最近ではエスカレーターでは歩行禁止なのですか？

The premise of escalator safety standards is that we are to use them without walking.

エスカレーターの安全基準は、歩かず利用することが前提です。

As there are people who cannot step to one side, such as those walking with canes, so railroad companies are asking people not to walk and to grasp the handrail.

杖の使用者など片側に寄ることができない人もいるので、鉄道会社は歩かずに手すりにつかまるよう呼びかけています。

□ prohibit
動 禁止する

□ premise 名 前提
□ safety standards
安全基準

□ cane 名 杖
□ grasp
動 〜をつかむ
□ handrail
名 手すり

駐車場での停め方
Parking in a Parking Lot

58

日本では当たり前の「駐車場でのバック入れ」だが、欧米では前入れバック出しが普通。なので、日本の駐車場は彼らの目には不思議に映るのだ！

英語で言うと？

駐車場：**parking lot**　バック駐車：**reverse parking**　物理的な：**physical**
構造的な：**structural**　均一の：**uniform**　内輪差：**difference in the pivot position**　斜め：**diagonal**

Photo: J.Jさんによる写真 AC からの写真

How do you park in parking lots in Japan?
日本では駐車場にどのように車を停めますか？

In Japan, reverse parking is the mainstream.

日本では、バック駐車が主流です。

At driving schools, time is spent practicing reverse parking and parallel parking.

自動車学校では、バック駐車や縦列駐車の習得に時間をかけます。

☐ parking lot
駐車場

☐ reverse parking
後ろ向きで入る並列
駐車

☐ parallel parking
縦列駐車

While it is partly due to the methodical temperament of Japanese people, there are physical reasons as well.

□ methodical
形 几帳面な
□ temperament
名 気質
□ physical
形 物理的な

日本人の几帳面な気質もありますが、物理的な理由もあります。

What kinds of reasons?
どんな理由ですか？

The reasons are mainly physical and structural.

□ structural
形 構造上の

おもに物理的および構造的な理由です。

In most cases, the spaces and the aisles at parking lots in Japan are narrow.

□ aisle 名 通路

日本の駐車場は1台分のスペースも通路の幅も狭い場合が多いです。

Therefore, doing reverse parking makes it easier to keep a uniform distance between cars.

□ uniform
形 不変の

隣との距離を均一に保つため、バック駐車の方が停めやすいからです。

What disadvantages are there to forward parking in Japan?
日本で車を頭から停めると、どのようなデメリットがありますか？

In the case of a narrow parking lot, there is a difference in the pivot position, and it is possible that you will come in contact with the car next to yours.

□ disadvantage
名 不利な立場
□ pivot
名 旋回軸；中心となるもの
□ in contact with
〜と接触して

狭い駐車場の場合、内輪差が発生し隣の車と接触する可能性があります。

It's also possible that your car will be turned so that it is not within the boundaries of the space, or that it will be diagonal.

□ boundary
名 境界線
□ diagonal
形 斜めの

駐車場の枠内に収まらずに曲がったり、ななめになってしまうことも考えられます。

THEME 59
100円ショップ
100-yen Shops

 59

今や日常生活に必須の"百均"。様々なアイテムがみっしり詰まった店内を、宝探し気分でご案内しましょう！

英語で言うと？ -------------------------------------

商品：**product** 均一：**flat; uniform** さまざまな：**various** 料金システム：**fee structure** 例外：**exception** 同様の：**similar**

Photo: 清十郎 / PIXTA (ピクスタ)

Why are 100-yen shops so popular in Japan?
100円ショップってどうして日本で人気なの？

Because everything in the shop can be bought for 100 yen.

店内の商品がすべて100円均一で購入できるからです。

They have many different items, from food to furniture.

食品から家具まで、さまざまなアイテムが揃います。

○ 江戸時代には「四文屋」とよばれる、何でも四文で買えるお惣菜の店があったらしい。また、アメリカでも、dollar stores などの価格が均一のお店がある。

Japan's first 100-yen shop opened in 1985 in Aichi Prefecture.

日本で最初の店舗型100円均一店は、1985年に愛知県でオープンしました。

What is the price system?
料金システムは？

 Generally, all items in the shop cost 100 yen, but there are some exceptions.

基本的に、店内にあるものはすべて100円ですが、中には例外もあります。

 There are also 88-yen and 99-yen shops.

88円ショップや、99円ショップもあります。

 Similarly, there are also 300-yen and 500-yen shops.

同じような形態で、300円、500円均一のお店もあります。

☐ exception
名 例外

 100円ショップ最大手のダイソーは、今やアジアやアメリカなどの海外での出店も実現している。

How can I enjoy a 100-yen shop?
どうやって楽しめばいいの？

 They also sell traditional Japanese items like paper fans or *tenugui* cloths, so they're a good place to buy souvenirs.

扇子や手ぬぐいなど、日本の伝統的な雑貨も取り扱っているので、お土産選びにもおすすめです。

 There are also shops that sell side dish items, so they might be good places to try some Japanese foods.

小分けにされたお惣菜を取り扱う店もあるので、日本食を少しだけ体験したいときにもいいかもしれません。

 They also sell things like umbrellas or T-shirts, so they're good for items you might need while traveling.

傘やＴシャツなども売っているので、旅行中に急に必要になったものをそろえるものいいでしょう。

☐ traditional
形 伝統的な

☐ souvenir 名 土産

THEME 60

ワークマン
Workman

 60

頑丈で機能的で、最近はおしゃれなデザインの製品も増えて注目されているワークマン。合理性を好むお客様に、ご提案してみると喜ばれるかも！

英語で言うと？

土木：**civil engineering**　工場：**factory**　農作業：**farming**
カジュアルウエア：**casual clothing**　作業着：**work clothes**　小物：**accessory**

Is Workman a popular shop in Japan?
ワークマンは日本で人気の店なの？

It is very popular among people who work in civil engineering and at factories.

土木作業や工場作業などの仕事をする人にとても人気です。

Recently there are items with cool designs, which are popular as casual clothing among young people.

最近はおしゃれなデザインのものがあり、若い人たちのカジュ

□ civil engineering
　土木工学

156

アルウエアとしても人気があります。

● The quality of the products has spread across Japan through social media, and it is also praised for its outdoor sports clothing.

□ spread across
　〜に散在する

商品のよさがSNSで日本中に広まり、アウトドアスポーツのウエアとしても好評です。

What kinds of products are there at Workman?
ワークマンにはどんな商品があるの？

● Work clothes and clothing that are easy for those working in civil engineering and factories to wear, and there are also many small items such as helmets.

土木作業や工場作業などがしやすい作業着やウエア、ヘルメットなどの小物もたくさんあります。

● And there are lots of clothes for working outside.

畑仕事用のウエアもたくさんあります。

● They also handle uniforms for office work as well as white coats to be worn in kitchens.

オフィス用の制服や調理場で着る白衣なども取り扱っています。

What are the special characteristics of them?
ワークマンにある商品の特徴は？

● They are made so people can work outdoors safely and comfortably on particularly hot or cold days, or on days when the weather is bad.

□ safely 副 安全に
□ comfortably
　副 気楽に

暑い日や寒い日も天気が悪い日も、屋外で安全に快適に活動できるようにつくられています。

● Despite being inexpensive, they are comfortable and durable.

□ despite
　前 〜にもかかわらず
□ durable
　形 耐久性のある

安いのに着心地がよくて丈夫なつくりです。

● They have both men's and women's clothing.

男性用と女性用があります。

157

THEME 61

かっぱ橋道具街
Kappabashi Tool Street

61

包丁やゴマすり器、玉子焼き器など、日本の調理器具も、外国人観光客に非常に人気があります。だったらここ！というのがかっぱ橋道具街です。

キッチン用具がなんでもそろう！ 訪日観光客にも大人気！

英語で言うと？

道具商：**shop by tool** 古物商：**antique merchant** 料理道具：**cooking utensil**
由来：**origin** 雨がっぱ：**raincoat** 水はけ：**drinage**

写真提供：(公財) 東京観光財団

What is "Kappabashi Dogu Gai"?
かっぱ橋道具街ってどんなところ？

Sparked by the opening in Taisho year 1 of shops by tool and antique merchants, it developed into a tool street offering everything including cooking utensils.

大正元年に道具商や古物商が店を出したことがきっかけで、料理道具がなんでもそろう道具街に発展しました。

□ utensil
名 (主に台所の) 器具

● The origin of the name Kappabashi is said to be in that *samurai* used to dry their raincoats, and that "kappa," or water imps, helped to ensure the area had good drainage.

かっぱ橋の名前の由来は、侍がこの地で雨がっぱを干していたこと、水はけのいい地域にするために河童（かっぱ）が手伝ったことと言われています。

● Kappabashi Dogu Gai, or Kappabashi Tool Street, is a street about 800 meters long with about 170 shops, where culinary professionals and common people can also shop.

かっぱ橋道具街は約800メートルの道に約170の店があり、プロの料理人も一般客も買い物ができます。

□ water imp　河童
□ **ensure**
　動 ～を守る；保証する
□ **drainage**
　名 水はけ

□ **culinary**
　形 料理の；台所の

Besides looking at and buying cooking utensils, are there other ways to enjoy the area?

料理道具を見る・買う以外に楽しみ方はある？

● You can experience making food product samples such as *tempura* and vegetables, and take them home as well.

天ぷらや野菜などの食品サンプルを作る体験ができ、持ち帰ることもできます。

● You can also take a commemorative photo next to Kappa Kawataro, a statue of a *kappa*, which was created in celebration of the 90th anniversary of the birth of Kappabashi Tool Street.

かっぱ橋道具街誕生90年を記念して建てられた、かっぱ河太郎と記念撮影もできます。

□ **anniversary**
　名 記念日

● Taking part in the Kappabashi Tool Matsuri, or festival, which takes place each fall, is also enjoyable.

毎年秋に実施される「かっぱ橋道具まつり」に参加するのも楽しいです。

□ **enjoyable**
　形 楽しい

くらし・習慣

THEME 62

中華街
Chukagai (Chinatown)

 62

欧米にもチャイナタウンはありますが、日本の中華街も依然として人気の
スポットです。中華まんを食べ歩きつつご案内なんていかがでしょう？

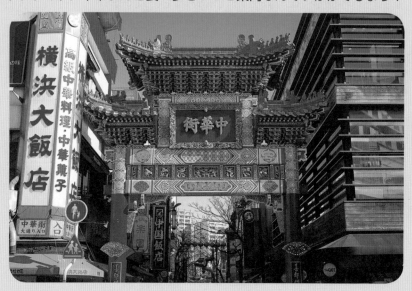

規模：**scale**　特徴：**characteristics**　平方メートル：**square meter**
華僑：**Chinese expatriate**　敷地：**site**　伝統文化：**traditional culture**

Photo: ポコポコさんによる写真 AC からの写真

Which of Japan's "Chukagai" is the most popular?

日本の中華街でいちばん有名なのはどこ？

Japan has three Chukagai, or Chinatowns,
and the largest one is Yokohama
Chukagai, which is in Yokohama City,
Kanagawa Prefecture.

日本には３つの中華街があり、いちばん規模が大きいのは神奈
川県横浜市にある横浜中華街です。

🗨️ Nankinmachi in Kobe City, Hyogo Prefecture is also one of Japan's Chukagai.

兵庫県神戸市にある南京町も日本の中華街の１つです。

🗨️ In Nagasaki City, Nagasaki Prefecture, there is Nagasaki Shinchi Chukagai.

長崎県長崎市にも長崎新地中華街（ながさきしんちちゅうかがい）という中華街があります。

What is the difference between Japan's three Chukagai?

日本にある３つの中華街の違いは何？

🗨️ On a site measuring about 500 meters square, Yokohama Chukagai has over 500 shops, the largest Chukagai in East Asia.

横浜中華街は500メートル四方の敷地に500以上の店があり、東アジア最大の中華街です。

□ site　名 敷地
□ measure　動 測る
🔸 square meter だと、「平方メートル」の意味になる

🗨️ Nankinmachi in Kobe has the most Chinese expatriates in Japan, and has over 100 shops on a site smaller than that of Yokohama Chukagai.

神戸の南京町は華僑の数が日本一多く、横浜中華街よりも狭い敷地に100以上の店があります。

□ expatriate
　名 国外居住者

🗨️ Nagasaki Shinchi Chukagai has the longest history as a Chukagai. It was created in cooperation with China's Fujian Province, and has around 40 shops.

長崎新地中華街はもっとも歴史が古く、中国の福建省と協力してつくった中華街で、店舗数は40程度です。

□ in cooperation
　with　〜と協議して

What are some popular spots in Chukagai?
中華街で人気のスポットは？

● Eating confectioneries or *manju* while walking are popular.

スイーツやまんじゅうなどの食べ歩きが人気です。

● There are also many tourists who visit places where the gods of China are enshrined.

中国の神様が祀られている（まつられている）場所を訪れる観光客も多いです。

□ enshrined
動 祀る

● この三大中華街に行く時間はないな…というお客様は、池袋駅北口エリアにある "池袋チャイナタウン" にお連れするのもおすすめ！

● At seasonal festivals and events, you can enjoy China's traditional culture.

季節のお祭りやイベントでは、中国の伝統文化を楽しむこともできます。

兵庫県神戸市中央区にある中華街「南京町」

162

THEME 63
築地場外市場
Tsukiji Outer Market

 63

築地市場は豊洲に移転しましたが、場外市場は依然として人気の観光地です。簡単な歴史や現状について、説明できるようにしておきましょう！

最近では英語での説明や英語メニューも完備されている

くらし・習慣

英語で言うと？

商店街：**commercial street**　住宅街：**residential area**　全焼する：**burn down**
水産物：**seafood**　取引量：**transaction volume**　関係者：**authorized people**

写真提供：(公財) 東京観光財団

How long has Tsukiji Outer Market been around?

築地場外市場はいつからあるの？

Sparked by the opening of Tsukiji Market in 1935, a commercial street was born, and this became today's Tsukiji Outer Market.

昭和10年に築地市場ができたことがきっかけで商店街が誕生し、現在の築地場外市場になりました。

☐ commercial street　商業街路

163

There used to be temples and a residential area on the site of Tsukiji Outer Market, but they all burned down in the Great Kanto Earthquake of 1923.

築地場外市場の場所は、もともと寺や住宅街などがありましたが、大正12年の関東大震災で全焼しました。

Before it became Tsukiji Outer Market, it was a bustling commercial street featuring things like barber shops and "sento," or public baths.

今の築地場外市場になる前は、床屋や銭湯などもある賑やかな商店街でした。

What's the difference between Tsukiji Outer Market and Tsukiji Market?

築地場外市場と築地市場は何が違うの？

Tsukiji Market was overseen and managed by the City of Tokyo and was one of the world's top markets in terms of seafood transaction volume, and had some places where only authorized people were able to make purchases.

築地市場は、東京都が「管理監督」していた水産物の取引量が世界最大級の市場で、関係者しか買い物できない場所がありました。

Anyone can freely enjoy shopping and dining at Tsukiji Outer Market.

築地場外市場では、一般客が自由に買い物や食事を楽しむことができます。

Tsukiji Market relocated to Toyosu, Koto Ward on October 11, 2018, but Tsukiji Outer Market continues operation in the same location.

築地市場は、2018年10月11日に江東区豊洲に移転しましたが、築地場外市場はそのまま営業しています。

Is Tsukiji Outer Market popular among Japanese people?

築地場外市場は日本人に人気があるの？

It is crowded with Japanese customers at year's end, purchasing ingredients in preparation for New Year's.

お正月を迎える準備で食材を買うために、年末は日本人客で混み合います。

Things like fresh seafood and "tamagoyaki," or Japanese rolled omelettes are popular with housewives.

主婦には、新鮮な海産物や卵焼きなども人気です。

There are also Japanese people who have favorite *sushi* or *ramen* shops there.

お気に入りの寿司店やラーメン店などがある日本人もいます。

□ ingredient
名 材料；要因
□ preparation
名 用意

□ rolled omelette
卵焼き
□ housewife
名 専業主婦

くらし・習慣

写真提供：(公財) 東京観光財団

165

THEME 64
日暮里繊維街
Nippori Textile Town

 64

昨今、世界中の手芸・裁縫好きのお客様が押し寄せているのが日暮里の繊維街。成田空港から直通電車で来られるのもポイントが高い！

英語で言うと？ ----------------------------------

古布：**recycled cloth**　はぎれ：**scrap**　布地：**fabric**　糸：**yarn**　手芸用品：**handicraft product**　手芸店：**handicraft shop**

Photo: YNS / PIXTA (ピクスタ)

How did "Nippori Senigai", or Nippori Textile Town, come to be?
どうして日暮里繊維街があるの？

It started early in the Taisho period, when sellers of recycled cloth and scraps of cloth relocated to Nippori from Asakusa.

大正時代初期に、古布やはぎれの商売人が浅草からここに移転したことが始まりです。

Merchants handling fabric and handicraft products gathered one after another, and it was around 1955 that it became what it is today.

布地や手芸用品を扱う商売人が次々に集まり、昭和30年ごろになって現在のようになりました。

☐ handicraft product
手工業製品
☐ one after another
次々に

There are more than 80 shops lined up on a street of about one kilometer.

1km くらいの通りに80以上の店が並んでいます。

Why are fabric and handicraft products inexpensive?

布や手芸用品が安いのはなぜ？

It is a wholesaler street where traders operating businesses such as handicraft shops purchase in bulk, so items can be purchased for less here than at general shops.

手芸店などの業者が大量に仕入れる問屋街なので、一般的な店よりも安く買えます。

☐ inexpensive
形 安価な

☐ wholesaler
名 問屋
☐ trader 名 商人
☐ in bulk 大量に

Various types of fabric, yarn, buttons, ribbons and just about every other textile material.

いろいろな種類の布、糸、ボタン、リボンなど、衣類の材料はなんでもあります。

☐ yarn 名 糸

For this reason, in the case of fabric, there are some shops that won't sell less than three meters.

そのため、布であれば3m 以上じゃないと買えない店舗などもあります。

Depending on the product, there are things that are not so inexpensive, but there aren't any items that are more expensive than at general shops.

商品によってはそれほど安くないものもありますが、一般的な店よりも高いものはありません。

くらし・習慣

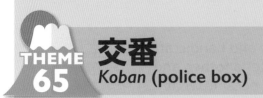

THEME 65
交番
Koban (police box)

 65

どんな時に交番を頼ればいいか、ご案内しておくのは大切です。最近では、外国語対応可能な職員が配置されている交番も出てきました。

英語で言うと？ --

警察官：**police officer**　警察署：**police station**　安全を守る：**preserve safety**
地域：**area**　24時間体制：**24 hours a day**　駐在所：**police substation**

Photo: オブキナさんによる写真 AC からの写真

Why are there "koban," or police boxes, in Japan?

日本にはどうして交番があるの？

The *koban* building first appeared in Tokyo in 1874, and spread across all of Japan.

交番の建物は明治7年に東京で誕生し、日本全国に広がっていきました。

168

● Before there were *koban* buildings, police officers would take turns going from the police station and preserving safety.

交番の建物がないころは、警察署から警察官が街に出て、交代で安全を守っていました。

● Without buildings, their activities are difficult on days when the weather is bad, so *koban* were built throughout cities.

建物がないと、天気が悪い日の活動が大変なので、街の中に交番をつくりました。

What does *koban* mean?
交番の意味は？

● It refers to a place where a number of police officers take turns keeping watch 24 hours a day in order to keep the area safe.

地域の安全を守るために、何人かの警察官が24時間体制で交代で番をする場所を言います。

☐ take turns　交代で

● At a "chuuzaijo," or police substation, which serves the same role as the *koban*, one or two police officers keep the area safe while also living there.

交番と同じ役割の駐在所は、1〜2人の警察官がそこに住みながら地域の安全を守っています。

☐ substation
　名 支署；支局

● Nationwide there are about 6,600 *koban*, and about 7,600 *chuuzaijo*.

全国に交番は約6600か所、駐在所は約7600か所あります。

What kinds of activities do police officers at a *koban* undertake?
交番はどのような活動をしているの？

💬 They respond when a crime or accident has occurred, or patrol the area.

事件や事故が起きたときの対応やパトロールなどをします。

💬 They also give directions, hold lost items, and offer consultation to people with problems.

道案内や落し物の取扱い、困り事の相談などもしています。

💬 There are also *koban* where one or more police officers speak a foreign language.

外国語を話せる警察官などが1名以上いる交番もあります。

☐ undertake
動 引き受ける

☐ respond 動 答える
☐ crime 名 犯罪

☐ give directions
道順を教える；指図する

☐ consultation
名 相談

日本独自の制度である交番制度は、「KOBAN」システムとして、米国の大学教授D・H・ベイリー氏によって紹介されたり、英語文献にもKOBANの表記が見られ、次第に国際語として市民権を得るようになり、そのため、ローマ字表記のKOBANであらわされているそうだ

国民皆保険
Universal Health Insurance

 66

保険制度は国ごとに様々です。外国人の中には、日本の保険に興味を持つ人が少なくありません。基本情報をお伝えできるよう準備しましょう。

くらし・習慣

英語で言うと？
- -

医療保険：**health insurance**　保険料：**insurance premium**　医療費：**medical cost**　自営業：**self-employed**　無職者：**unemployed**　後期高齢者：**latter-stage elderly**

Photo: soraraさんによる写真ACからの写真

Why does everyone in Japan enroll in health insurance?

日本人はなぜ全員が医療保険に入るの？

Because in 1958, the National Health Insurance Act was enacted, where everyone in the country enrolls in some form of health insurance at fixed rates.

1958年に全国民はなんらかの医療保険に加入し、一定の保険料を支払う国民健康保険法が定められたからです。

☐ enroll in
　（大学などに）入る

☐ health insurance
　健康保険

☐ National Health
　Insurance Act
　国民健康保険法

☐ enact 　動 制定する

171

The regulation was born of a desire to help each other, and so that people would not have the burden of various medical costs when illness or injury occurred.

病気やけがをしたときに多額の医療費を負担しなくて済むように、助け合いの気持ちから生まれた制度です。

Before the National Health Insurance Act was enacted, about one in three citizens were not enrolled in health insurance.

国民健康保険法ができる前は国民の約3分の1が保険未加入でした。

Some people could not receive medical examinations because they could not pay the medical costs, and it became a societal problem.

医療費が払えずに受診できない人がいて、社会問題になっていました。

Are there different types of health insurance?
医療保険には種類があるの？

Company employees enroll in health insurance, while government employees enroll in mutual aid associations.

会社員は健康保険、公務員などは共済組合に加入します。

People who work on farms, are self-employed, or are unemployed, enroll in national health insurance.

農業に従事する人、自営業者、無職者などは国民健康保険に加入します。

Once we reach the age of 75, we enroll in the latter-stage elderly healthcare system.

75歳以上になると、後期高齢者医療制度に加入します。

□ regulation
　名 規制；規則

□ burden　名 負担

□ medical examination
　診察；健康診断
□ societal problem
　社会問題

□ company employee　会社員
□ government employee　公務員
□ mutual aid association
　共済組合

□ self-employed
　自営業者
□ unemployed
　形 失業中の
　名 失業者

□ healthcare system　医療制度

Do you pay insurance premiums even when you are not ill or injured?

病気やケガをしていないときも保険料を支払うの？

Yes, each month we pay an amount commensurate with our income, even if we are not ill or injured.

病気やケガをしていなくても、収入に見合った保険料を毎月支払います。

The number of low-income people is increasing, as are the number of people who don't enroll in health insurance or don't pay insurance premiums.

収入が少ない人が増え、医療保険に加入しない人や保険料を払わない人も増えています。

The continued aging of enrollees and the subsequent operational deficit for health insurance has become a problem in Japan.

加入者の高齢化が進み、医療保険の運営が赤字であることも日本では問題になっています。

□ insurance premium 保険料

□ commensurate
形 等しい；釣り合った
□ income 名 収入

□ low-income
低所得の

□ enrollee
名 入学者
□ subsequent
形 次の
□ operational
形 使用可能な；運営の
□ deficit
名 赤字額；損失

くらし・習慣

173

THEME 67
ゲンかつぎ、ジンクス
Genkatsugi (superstition, jinx)

🔽 67

日本独特のゲン担ぎを面白がる外国人は多いです。もちろん日本以外にも
「縁起」的な事物はありますので比較して楽しむのも一興ですね！

幸運のシンボル！　四つ葉のクローバー

英語で言うと？
- -

ゲンかつぎ：**superstition**　希少性：**rarity**　洗面台：**sink**　水回り：**plumbing-related thing**　爪を切る：**clip nail**

Photo: KIKU29qさんによる写真 AC からの写真

What is "genkatsugi"?
ゲンかつぎとはなんですか？

😃 It used to be "engikatsugi," but changed to *genkatsugi*.

「縁起かつぎ」が変化して「ゲンかつぎ」となりました。

😃 That's why it means the same thing as *engikatsugi*.

そのため、意味は「縁起かつぎ」と同じです。

174

What kinds of famous superstitions are there?

有名なゲンかつぎにはどんなものがありますか？

● Walking around with a four-leaf clover, the rarity of which has value.

希少価値のある四葉のクローバーを持ち歩くこと。

● Another is keeping plumbing-related things like sinks and toilets clean.

洗面台やトイレなど水回りをきれいに保つこと。

● Yet another is not clipping nails at night.

夜に爪を切らないこと、などがあります。

□ rarity
名 まれなこと [もの]；希少性

□ value
名 価値；値打ち

□ plumbing
名 配管；水道設備

□ clip nails
爪を切る

Why don't you clip your nails at night?

夜に爪を切らない理由はなんですか？

● We don't clip our nails at night because there's an expression, "yozume," which means that it leads to a shortened life.

夜に爪を切ることは、その語感から「世詰め（よづめ）」をあらわす行為、とされています。

● "Yozume" means that you will not be able to see the death of your parents.

「世詰め」とは、親の死に目に会えなくなる、という意味です。

● In essence, it means that your life will end before that of your parents, so that may be why many Japanese people don't clip their nails at night.

つまり親よりも自分が先に死んでしまう、ということを意味するため、夜に爪を切らない日本人は多いかもしれません。

□ in essence
本当のところ；実は

縁起
Engi (luck)

日本の縁起かつぎは往々にして「語呂合わせ（というかダジャレ？）」が元になっていることが多いので、説明すると面白がってもらえるかも！

ゼッタイ勝つ！と気合の語呂合わせごはん！

英語で言うと？

吉凶：**fortune**　前兆：**sign**　前ぶれ：**warning**　起源：**origin**　ささいな：**petty**
重視する：**focus on**

Photo: キキくんさんによる写真 AC からの写真

What does "engi" mean?
縁起とはどういう意味ですか？

It refers to a harbinger or warning. It is also used to refer to the start or origin of things.

吉凶の前兆や前ぶれのことです。物ごとの起源や由来をさすこともあります。

☐ harbinger
　名 前触れ；先駆者
☐ warning
　名 （悪いことの）前兆；警告

In Japan, we tend to worry about whether there are good signs or bad signs with regard to little things.

日本ではささいな物事に対して、よい前兆なのか悪い前兆なのかを気にしがちです。

For this reason, we repeat actions that in the past had good results, and hope for good results again this time.

そのため、以前よい結果が出た行為を繰り返し行い、今回のよい結果を期待するのです。

In what situations do you focus on luck?
どんなときに縁起を重視しますか？

On the day before a test, on the day a wedding is scheduled, or when we visit someone in the hospital.

受験前日や結婚式の日取り、入院患者へのお見舞いなどです。

We eat "katsudon" ("katsu" also means "win") when we want to pass a test, or select a "good day" based on old calendar fortune telling.

受験に勝つよう「カツ丼」を食べたり、昔の暦占いに基づいた「よい日」を選んだりします。

We avoid giving potted plants as gifts to hospital patients because it conveys the image of "taking root in the hospital."

入院患者への手土産は「病院に根付く」というイメージがあるため鉢植えを避けます。

☐ potted plant
鉢植えの植物
☐ patient 名 患者
☐ take root in
（植物や習慣が）〜に
根付く

What kinds of lucky charms are there?

どんな縁起物がありますか？

In terms of familiar things, it is considered good luck to have a tea leaf stem standing in your teacup.

身近なものでは、湯のみに茶葉の茎である茶柱が立っていることです。

This is because it is unusual for a tea leaf stem to get through the mesh of the teapot into the teacup.

茶葉の茎が急須の網の目をくぐり、湯のみに入ることは珍しいからです。

Moreover, as it is even more unusual for a stem to "stand," we have come to believe this is a good sign.

そのうえ「立つ」のはさらに珍しいため、よい知らせ、と考えられるようになりました。

□ familiar
形 身近な
□ stem 名 茎

穴のあいたコイン
Coins with Holes in them

 69

穴があいているコインが珍しいと言う訪日観光客はけっこう多いのです。
初めて日本の硬貨を目にした人には一通り説明してあげましょう。

英語で言うと？ -

穴があいている：**have a hole**　節約：**conserve**　偽造防止：**counterfeit prevention**　〜を参考にする：**usa 〜 for reference**　特別な使い方：**special usage**　金運：**fortune related to money**

Why do the five-yen and fifty-yen coins have holes in them?

5円と50円玉はなぜ穴があいているの？

💬 The reason the five-yen coin has a hole in it is to conserve materials.

5円玉に穴があいているのは、材料を節約するためです。

☐ conserve
動 〜節約する

くらし・習慣

The reason the fifty-yen coin has a hole in it is to prevent it from being confused with the one-hundred-yen coin.

50円玉に穴があいているのは、100 円玉と間違えないようにするためです。

□ confuse
動 混同する

The five- and fifty-yen coins also have holes in them for "gizouboushi," or counterfeit prevention.

５円玉も50円玉も穴があいているのは 偽造防止（ぎぞうぼうし）のためでもあります。

□ counterfeit
名 偽造（品）
□ prevention
名 防止

Has Japan had coins with holes in them since long ago?

日本には昔から穴のあいたコインがあるの？

The first coin in Japan that had a hole in it was made in the year 683.

日本で初めて穴のあいたコインが作られたのは683年。

It was the "fumonsen," produced using a Chinese coin for reference.

中国のコインを参考に造られた「富本銭（ふもんせん）」です。

□ for reference
参考のために

The first coin with a hole in it to be used in Japan was the "wadokaichin" in the year 708.

穴のあいたコインが日本で初めて使われたのは、708年に誕生した「和同開珎（わどうかいちん）」です。

The present-day five-yen coin first appeared in August 1949, and the fifty-yen coin in 1967.

現在の５円玉は 昭和24年８月に、50円玉は昭和42年に誕生しました。

□ present-day
形 今日の

Do coins with holes in them have a special usage?

穴のあいたコインは特別な使い方があるの？

● Five- and fifty-yen coins are said to have better "engi," or luck, than other coins.

5円玉と50円玉は、ほかのコインよりも縁起（えんぎ）がいいと言われています。

● When doing "sanpai," or worshipping, at a shrine or temple, these coins are commonly put into the "saisenbako," or offertory box.

神社や寺の参拝（さんぱい）で賽銭箱（さいせんばこ）に入れる人が多いです。

● Before using a new wallet, if we put a five-yen coin into it, it is said our fortune related to money will improve.

新しいお財布を使う前に5円玉を入れておくと、金運が上がると言われています。

□ worship
動 崇拝する

□ offertory box
献金箱

□ fortune 名 (幸)運
□ relate to
〜にかかわる

くらし・習慣

穴あきコインの1つ、五円玉には、表にも裏にも数字が書かれていないので、日本語がわからない人にはそれがいくらなのかがわかりません。「五」の字が「5」を意味することも併せてご案内すると親切です

Photo: sasaki106 / PIXTA (ピクスタ)

181

THEME 70 数の数え方
How to Count Numbers

🔽 70

指を使って、「正」の字を使って、「ぼん」と 「ほん」と 「ぽん」の違い…など
など、日本の数え方は外国人の目には独特に映るようです。

オーソドックスなお札の数え方

英語で言うと？ -

順番に：**in order**　指をたてる：**raise one's finger**　指を折る：**fold one's finger**
札をめくる：**peeling the bills**　文字：**character**　画数：**strokes**

Photo: freeangle / PIXTA (ピクスタ)

In Japan, when counting using your fingers, what do you do?
日本では指を使って数を数えるとき、どうしますか？

😊 We raise our fingers in order beginning
with the index finger, and ending with
the thumb.

人差し指から順番に指を立て、最後に親指で終わります。

☐ index finger
　人差し指
☐ thumb 　名 親指

182

In some cases, we count starting with our hands open, then fold our fingers inward, starting with the thumb.

□ inward 副 内側へ

手を開いた状態から、親指から順に内側に折って数える場合もあります。

In America, France, and Germany, they start with the thumb and raise the fingers in order, but in Taiwan they count starting with the pinkie.

□ pinkie 名 小指

アメリカやフランス、ドイツは親指から順に指をたてて、台湾は小指から数えます。

What do you do when counting a bundle of bills?

札束を数えるときはどうしますか？

Most people secure the bundle of bills in one hand, while peeling the bills with the other hand and counting them.

□ bundle of bills 札束

□ secure 動 〜を固定する

□ peel 動 はがす

片手で札束を固定し、もう片方の手でめくって数えることが多いです。

Depending on the type of work and age, in some cases we shift the bills from our right hand to our left hand and count them one at a time.

□ shift 動 変える；移す

職業や年齢にもよりますが、紙幣を右手から左手に移して１枚ずつ数える場合もあります。

Professionals such as people who work at banks spread the bills into a fan shape and count quickly.

銀行員などのプロは、扇形に札束を広げ素早く数えます。

くらし・習慣

Are there cases where you count using *kanji* characters in place of symbols?

漢字を記号代わりにして数を数える場合もあるのですか？

We count using the character 正 (*sei*).

「正」の字を使って数を数えます。

The character 正 has five strokes, so completing the character means we have counted to five.

「正」の字は5画でできているので、1文字完成すると5カウントされたことになります。

This is used in situations such as counting votes at school.

学校で投票数を数えるときなどに使います。

□ stroke
名 一筆の動き

□ vote
名 票；投票（結果）

Chapter 3

外国人がいちばん不思議に思う
日本の食文化

お次はみんな大好き日本の味！ といっても、高価で
豪華なフォーマル和食ではなく、どちらかというと我々
の日常に地続きの食文化──しかも外国人の目からは不
思議に映る──について、英語で説明してみましょう！

FOOD CULTURE

THEME 71
そば
Soba

日本式の蕎麦は、その多様な食べ方や薬味など、外国人にとっては「初体験」ばかり。蕎麦打ち体験へのご案内も視野に、英語で説明しましょう。

せいろに盛られたざるそば

英語で言うと？

漬け汁：**dipping sauce**　生卵：**raw egg**　油揚げ：**deep-fried tofu**
定年退職者：**retiree**　高齢者：**elderly**　体験：**experience**

Photo: raining_photo さんによる写真 AC からの写真

How do you eat *soba*?
そばはどのように食べますか？

Noodles made with buckwheat flour are often blended with regular white flour.

そば粉で作られる麺ですが、多くの場合は小麦粉とブレンドされます。

It is served cold with a dipping sauce, and we also eat it warm with a warm soup.

冷たくして漬け汁と一緒に出したり、温かくして熱い汁に入れて食べたりします。

☐ blend
　名 混ぜること；混合
☐ buckwheat
　名 蕎麦

186

😊 We put many different toppings on it, such as *tempura*, raw egg, and deep-fried *tofu*.

天ぷら、生卵、油揚げなど、いろいろなトッピングをのせることもあります。

What does "soba uchi" mean?
そば打ちってなんですか？

😊 It describes the making of *soba* noodles from flour.

粉からそばを作ることです。

☐ describe
動 〜を述べる

😊 The action of "hitting" is part of the way of making it, so that's why it's called "soba uchi."

その作り方に「打つ」動作があるためこのように言われています。

😊 It is popular as a hobby among retirees and the elderly in Japan.

日本の定年退職者や高齢者層の趣味として人気です。

☐ retiree 名 退職者
☐ elderly 名 高齢者

Can we experience *soba* making?
そば打ちの体験はできますか？

😊 Domestically, there are a number of classrooms where you can experience *soba* making.

日本国内には、いくつかそば打ち体験できる教室があります。

😊 You can take home the *soba* you made — it's the perfect souvenir.

自分で打ったそばを持ち帰れるのでお土産にもぴったりです。

😊 There are classrooms where they explain in English, so please give it a try.

英語で説明してくれる教室もあるので、ぜひトライしてください。

ラーメン
Ramen

THEME 72

🔽 72

ramenは、すでに多くの国で通じる英単語です。日本の多様多彩なラーメンを目的に来日される方も多いです。ラーメン博物館はおすすめ！

シンプルな中華そば

英語で言うと？

ネギ：**green onion** つぶしたニンニク：**crushed garlic** 海苔：**dried seaweed**
スープ：**soup** 味付け：**seasoning** 麺の太さ **thickness of noodles**

Photo: 月舟さんによる写真 AC からの写真

Did *ramen* come from China?

ラーメンは中国から来たのでしょうか。

🗨 *Ramen* was originally a Chinese noodle
dish, but was developed into an original
dish in Japan.

ラーメンは中国の麺料理が起源で、日本で独自の進化を遂げました。

188

🍜 Japan's first *ramen* shop was in Asakusa.

「日本初のラーメン店」は浅草にありました。

🍜 That shop is no longer in business.

その店は、もう営業していません。

How many types of *ramen* are there.

ラーメンにはどれくらいの種類がありますか。

🍜 There's a Ramen Museum. They say there are 19 regional *ramen* styles.

ラーメン博物館というものがあります。そこでは19のご当地ラーメンがあると言われています。

🍜 You can add toppings like sesame seeds, green opnions and crushed garlic.

トッピングとして、ゴマやネギ、ニンニクなどを加えられます。

☐ green opnion
ネギ

☐ crushed garlic
おろしにんにく

🍜 If you finish your noodles before the soup, you can sometimes order extra noodles.

スープがまだあるのに麺を食べ終わってしまったら、追加で麺を注文できる場合もあります。

I'd love to be able to eat *ramen* at a famous restaurant.

有名店のラーメンを食べてみたいなあ

🍜 There are famous *ramen* shops all over Japan.

日本各地に有名なラーメン店があります。

🍜 Recently, cup *ramen* that reproduces the flavors of those famous *ramen* shops has become available at convenience stores.

最近では、そうした有名ラーメン店の味をカップラーメンで再現したものがコンビニで売られています。

☐ reproduce
動 ～を再生する

🍜 As we can easily enjoy the flavors of those shops, it might be fun to try them.

手軽に名店の味が楽しめるので、試すのも楽しいかもしれません。

食
文
化

189

インスタントラーメン
Instant *Ramen*

 73

インスタントラーメンは、軽くて安くてコンパクトですし、ご当地商品も
多く出ていますので、お土産としておすすめしてみましょう。

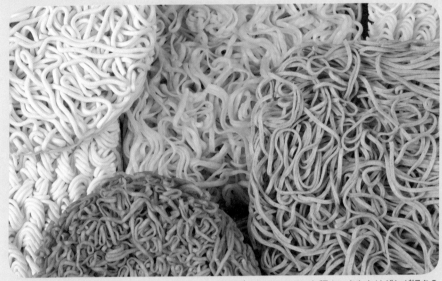

さまざまなインスタント麺！　あなたはどれが好き？

英語で言うと？------------------------------------

発明する：**invent**　製造方法：**production method**　年間の：**annual**　消費する：
consume　宇宙食：**space food**　無重力空間：**weightless environment**

Photo: セーラム / PIXTA（ピクスタ）

When was instant *ramen* born?
インスタントラーメンはいつ生まれたのですか？

🧑 Momofuku Ando, the founder of Nisshin
Food Products, invented it in 1958.

1958年に日清食品創業者の安藤百福が発明しました。

🧑 The cooking method came to him when
he was watching his wife deep frying
tempura.

彼の妻がてんぷらを揚げる様子を見て調理法を思いつきました。

□ founder
名 創設者

😀 At the time, chicken was the only instant *ramen* flavor.

当時はチキン味のインスタントラーメンのみでした。

 ## How much instant *ramen* is eaten in Japan?
日本ではインスタントラーメンをどれくらい食べますか？

😀 The annual volume consumed is nearly 5.8 billion portions.

年間の消費量は58億食近くになります。

□ consume
動 消費する
□ billion 名 10億

😀 That works out to about 43 portions per citizen per year.

国民1人当たり、約43食を1年間に食べていることになります。

😀 Looking at annual consumption, Korea is first at 74.7 portions, with Vietnam second at 53.9, and Nepal third at 53. Japan ranks fifth.

年間消費量では、1位韓国74.7食、2位ベトナム53.9食、3位ネパール53食でした。日本は5位です。

🔵 このあたりの数字は年々変わるので、最新情報を check！

 ## Is it also consumed in space?
宇宙食にもなっているんですか？

😀 In July 2005, it was provided aboard the International Space Station.

2005年7月に、国際宇宙ステーションで提供されました。

□ International Space Station
国際宇宙ステーション

😀 It was developed jointly by Nisshin Food Products and the Japan Aerospace Exploration Agency (JAXA).

日清食品と宇宙航空研究開発機構（JAXA）によって開発されました。

□ jointly 副 合同で
□ Japan Aerospace Exploration Agency (JAXA)
宇宙航空研究開発機構

😀 It was designed for rehydration at 70 degrees Celsius so it won't scatter in a weightless environment.

摂氏70度で戻せ、無重量空間で飛び散らないよう工夫されています。

□ rehydration
名 再水和；水分補給
□ degrees Celsius
セ氏温度
□ scatter 動 ばらまく
□ weightless environment
無重力環境

191

カップラーメン
Cup *Ramen*

⬇ 74

有名ラーメン店の味を再現したカップ麺がたくさん出ていますので、実店舗の思い出を、ぜひお土産としておすすめしてみましょう！

英語で言うと？

専用の容器：**special container**　　人質事件：**hostage incident**　　生中継する：**live broadcast**　　機動隊員：**riot police**　　湯気が立つ：**steam billows out**

Photo: 胡麻油さんによる写真 AC からの写真

When was cup *ramen* born?
カップラーメンはいつ生まれたのですか？

🙂 Cup *ramen* was developed by the developer of instant *ramen*, Momofuku Ando, in 1971.

カップラーメンは、インスタントラーメンの開発者・安藤百福が1971年に発売しました。

🔵 The idea came to him out of the blue when he was in Europe and the US selling instant *ramen*.

欧米に即席ラーメンのセールスに行った際、思いつきました。

□ out of the blue
　思いがけなく；突然

🔵 He didn't have a container for *ramen* handy, so he portioned it into paper cups — this was how cup *ramen* was born.

その場にラーメン用の容器がなく、紙コップにチキンラーメンを割り入れて試食したことから誕生しました。

□ handy
　形 手元にある
□ portion
　動 ～を分割する

Why has cup *ramen* become popular?
カップラーメンが人気になった理由は何ですか？

🔵 In February 1972, the Asama-Sanso incident, a famous hostage crisis, took place.

1972年2月に有名な立てこもり事件「あさま山荘事件」がありました。

□ incident
　名 出来事；事件
□ hostage crisis
　人質事件

🔵 Images of this were broadcast live on television over the course of several days.

その様子がテレビで何日間にもわたり生中継されていました。

□ over the course of ～の間に；～にわたって

🔵 It was cold out, and the images of the riot police eating cup *ramen* with steam billowing out of it were shown repeatedly.

寒い中、機動隊員が湯気の出ているカップラーメンを食べる姿がなんども映し出されました。

□ riot police
　(暴動鎮圧の) 機動隊
□ billow out
　(煙が) もうもうと吹き出す
□ repeatedly
　副 繰り返して

🔵 It is said that this is how the public became aware of it.

そのため、国民に広まったと言われています。

□ public 名 国民

THEME 75

冷たい麺
Cold Noodles

最も知られる日本の麺料理＝ラーメンは大体熱い状態で食べます。暑さで
食欲が落ちる夏に、冷たく多彩な麺料理を紹介すると、驚き喜ばれます！

日本の夏と言えば…の代表例それは冷た〜いそうめん！

英語で言うと？

暑い季節：**warm seasons**　　のど越し：**feeling of food or drink going down one's throat**　　たれに浸ける：**dip in sauce**　　すする：**slurp**　　独自の進化：**unique evolution**

Are noodles chilled and eaten in Japan?
日本では麺類を冷やして食べますか？

Yes, there is a culture concerning eating cold noodles in Japan.

はい、日本には冷たい麺類を食べる文化があります。

Particularly during hot seasons when we don't have an appetite, we like cold noodles as they go down easy.

□ concern
動 （〜にとって）重要
である

□ appetite　名 食欲

194

とくに暑い季節などに食欲がないとき、のど越しの良い冷たい麺が好まれます。

 There is the type where we dip chilled noodles in sauce or *tsuyu*, and the type where we eat noodles already swimming in sauce or *tsuyu*.

冷やした麺をタレやつゆに浸けて食べるタイプと、冷やしたタレやつゆに浸かった状態で食べるタイプがあります。

What type is popular?
どんなものが人気ですか？

 Among the most popular is Japanese *soba*. Making a slurping noise while you eat makes it taste even better.

ポピュラーなものに、日本そばがあります。音をたててすすって食べると美味しさが増します。

□ slurp
動 音をたてて飲食する

 Hiyashi chuuka, where we chill and eat Chinese noodles, is also very common.

中華麺を冷やして食べる「冷やし中華」も一般的です。

 Recently, there is also *hiyashi ramen*, where we chill and eat *ramen*.

最近では、ラーメンを冷やした「冷やしラーメン」もあります。

食文化

Does it have a long history?
歴史は古いのですか？

 Noodles that came from China evolved, and during the Muromachi period, they became thinner to be eaten chilled in dishes like *somen* and *hiyamugi*.

中国から伝わった麺が進化し、室町時代には、そうめんやひやむぎなど、冷やして食べるため細くなりました。

 The present-day style of eating *soba* was established around the Edo period.

そばの食べ方が、現在のようなスタイルに定着したのは江戸時代ごろです。

THEME 76

カレー（ルー／レトルト）
Curry (roux, readymade)

76

カレーもまた、日本で独自に進化した食べ物で、訪日客は興味しんしん。
具材はもちろんトッピングや辛さの調整など、選択肢は無限ですね！

英語で言うと？

改良する：**improve**　粉末の：**powdered**　固形の：**solid**　液体の：**liquid**
家庭料理：**home-cooked dish**　ルー：**roux**

Photo: Fururun さんによる写真 AC からの写真

Is Japanese curry different from Indian curry?
日本のカレーはインドカレーとは違うのですか？

Indian curry was introduced to England
in the 18th century, and then came from
England to Japan during the Meiji Era.

インドのカレーは、18世紀にイギリスに伝わり、日本へは明治
時代にイギリスから入ってきました。

Powdered curry roux was developed during the Taisho Era, improving it so it was easier for Japanese people to make.

日本人は作りやすいように改良して、大正時代に粉末のカレールーを開発しました。

☐ powdered
形 粉末の
☐ roux 名 ルウ

 In 1950, solid curry roux first appeared, and curry with a unique stickiness rapidly spread as a home-cooked dish.

1950年には、固形のカレールーが登場し、独特の粘り気のあるカレーが、家庭料理として急速に広がりました。

☐ solid 形 固体の
☐ stickiness
名 粘性
☐ home-cooked
家庭で料理した

Has curry penetrated Japan's food culture?

日本人の食文化には、カレーが浸透しているのですか？

 There are many types of curry roux on display at supermarkets.

スーパーには、いろんな種類のカレールーが並んでいます。

☐ penetrate
動 〜に浸透する；入る

 There are many foods with curry flavoring, such as curry buns, curry-flavored snacks, and curry *udon*.

カレーパンやカレー味のスナック、カレーうどんなど、いろいろなものがカレー味にアレンジされています。

 Curry is always a popular item in school lunches and at fast-food restaurants.

学校給食やファストフード店でも、カレーはつねに人気メニューです。

食
文
化

Photo: ささざわ / PIXTA (ピクスタ)

197

Are there original, local curries in each of the 47 prefectures?

47都道府県それぞれに、オリジナルのご当地カレーがあるのですか？

● Readymade curry, which can be eaten by warming in water or heating in a microwave oven, is popular as a simple souvenir.

お湯で温めたり、電子レンジで加熱するだけで食べられる「レトルトカレー」は手軽なお土産としても人気があります。

● Local curries featuring famous produce from each region are very trendy lately.

最近では、地域ごとの名産を活かした「ご当地カレー」がブームになっています。

● Interest is apparently being stimulated by collaborations with famous produce from various regions of Japan, such as oysters and beef tongue.

牡蠣や牛タンなど、日本各地の名産とカレーのコラボレーションに好奇心を刺激されるようです。

☐ warm
動 ～をあたためる
☐ heat
動 ～を熱くする
☐ microwave oven
電子レンジ

☐ trendy
形 最新流行の

☐ collaboration
名 協力；共同制作

ご当地カレーの筆頭格の
1つ、スープカレー

冷たいお茶
Cold Tea

暑い時期に冷た〜いお茶類を飲む習慣も、外国人からすると珍しいと感じます。日本料理をご案内する際には、添えてご提案したいものですね。

水まんじゅうや水ようかんなどのお菓子も、涼しい気分をもたらしてくれる

食文化

英語で言うと?

冷やした：**chilled**　普及する：**spread**　飲料メーカー：**beverage manufacturer**
ペットボトル：**PET bottle**　独自の様式：**unique style**　茶道：**tea ceremony**

Do people drink cold tea in Japan?
日本では冷たいお茶を飲みますか？

In Japan, there is the custom of drinking chilled tea such as cold *matcha* and cold tea, particularly during hot periods.

日本には、冷抹茶、冷茶など、とくに暑い時期に冷やしたお茶を飲む風習があります。

□ chilled　形 冷蔵の

199

🫖 Generally sugar and milk are not added; it is drunk straight.

砂糖やミルクを加えず、ストレートで飲むのが一般的です。

🫖 Due to the spread to convenience stores and the efforts of beverage manufacturers, tea in PET bottles has spread.

☐ PET bottle
ペットボトル

コンビニエンスストアの普及と、飲料メーカーの努力で、ペットボトル入りのお茶が普及しています。

In what situations do they drink cold tea?

どんな場面で冷たいお茶を飲みますか？

🫖 Tea, which came from China together with Buddhism, had a unique style of tea ceremony created due to the influence of Zen thinking.

☐ tea ceremony
茶道
☐ influence 名 影響

中国から仏教とともに伝わったお茶は、禅思想の影響も受けながら、茶の湯として独自の様式に作り上げられました。

🫖 To prepare with one's warmest wishes, and to cherish the time spent together.

☐ warmest wishes
心をこめて
☐ cherish
動 〜を大事にする

客人のために心を込めて準備をし、共に過ごす時間を大切にする。

🫖 That is the foundation of the tea ceremony.

☐ foundation
名 土台；根幹

それが茶道の基本です。

🫖 Naturally we serve it to visitors during hot periods such as this, but cold tea has also become an essential part of everyday life.

☐ essential
形 絶対必要な；本質の

今では暑い時期の来客にはもちろん、普段の生活にも冷たいお茶は欠かせないものです。

Is there any trick to making delicious cold tea?

冷茶をおいしくいれるコツはありますか？

There are many ways to make cold green tea.

緑茶で冷茶を作るには、いろいろな方法があります。

The most common method is to put tea leaves and water in a teapot and chill them in the refrigerator.

一般的なものは、ティーポットに茶葉と水を入れ、冷蔵庫で冷やす方法です。

There is also a fancy method where we put ice on top of the tea leaves in the teapot, and extract flavor as the ice melts.

急須に入れた茶葉の上に氷をのせ、ゆっくり溶かしながら抽出する、というぜいたくな方法もあります。

□ extract
動 引き抜く；抽出する

ひと口に「日本茶」といってもいろいろな種類がありますね。コンビニで買える冷たいお茶の種類も年々増えています

Photo: freeangle / PIXTA (ピクスタ)

缶コーヒー
Canned Coffee

 78

あまりにも当たり前すぎるものですが、缶コーヒーは外国人の目には面白く映るようです。もちろん、試飲して大好きになる人続出！です！

英語で言うと？

駅の売店：**train station shop**　瓶入り：**bottled**　コーヒー牛乳：**coffee-flavored milk**　1人あたり：**per person**　焙煎：**roasting**　期間限定：**limited-time**

Where was canned coffee born?
缶コーヒーはどこで生まれたのですか？

The canned coffee with the longest history that is still being produced is UCC Coffee, first sold in Japan in April 1969.

現在も製造されているなかで最も歴史のある缶コーヒーは、1969年4月に日本で発売された「UCCコーヒー」です。

What sparked the birth of canned coffee was when people were drinking bottled coffee-flavored milk at train station shops.

缶コーヒーが生まれたきっかけは、駅の売店で瓶入りコーヒー牛乳を飲んでいたときです。

At the time, bottles needed to be returned to the shop, so the first canned coffee made its world debut as it could be enjoyed anytime, anywhere.

当時は瓶を店に返さねばならなかったため、いつでもどこでも手軽に、と、世界初の缶コーヒーが誕生しました。

About how much canned coffee do Japanese people drink?
日本人はどれくらい缶コーヒーを飲みますか？

Japanese people drink 95 cans of coffee per person per year.

日本人は、1人当たり年間95本の缶コーヒーを飲んでいます。

The spread to convenience stores and vending machines also played a part in Japan's canned coffee culture.

コンビニと自販機の普及も、その文化普及に一役買っています。

What types of canned coffee are there?
缶コーヒーにはどんな種類がありますか？

Domestically at present, there are more than 30 canned coffee manufacturers, producing over 300 types of canned coffee.

現在日本国内には缶コーヒーメーカーが30以上あり、その種類は300種類以上にのぼります。

☐ domestically
   副 国内で
☐ at present
   今のところ

There are also limited-time packaging and products limited to certain regions.

期間限定のパッケージや地域限定商品などもあります。

☐ packaging
   名 梱包すること

THEME 79 生卵を食べること
Eating Raw Eggs

79

卵料理はどの国でもあるでしょうが、世界的にも珍しい食べ方を、日本人は日常的に実践しています。その背景も含めてご案内しましょう。

英語で言うと？

専用の：**especially for**　こだわりの卵：**finest eggs**　専門化する：**specialize**　賞味期限：**expiration date**　品質管理：**quality management**　衛生管理：**hygiene management**

Photo: りこことさんによる写真 AC からの写真

What are some popular egg dishes in Japan?
日本での人気の卵料理はなんですか？

One is "tamagokakegohan," where we put a raw egg on top of freshly cooked rice.

生卵を炊きたてのごはんにかけて食べる「卵かけごはん」です。

There are also seasonings and cooking utensils especially for this.

専用の調味料や調理器具もあります。

□ freshly　副 新鮮に

□ seasoning
名 薬味；味付けするもの

There are restaurants that specialize in *tamagokakegohan* using the finest eggs.

こだわりの卵を使った卵かけご飯の専門店もあります。

Is it safe to eat a raw egg?

生で卵を食べても大丈夫なのですか？

Japan is very thorough regarding expiration dates and quality management.

日本では賞味期限や品質管理が徹底されています。

Based on proprietary hygiene management, they are shipped with no bacteria.

独自の衛生管理のもと、菌の付いていない状態で出荷されます。

Using extremely safe items all the way from chick feed, management is strict, so raw eggs can safely be eaten.

ヒナの飼料から安全性の高いものを使用し、厳しく管理されているため安心して生で食べることができます。

☐ thorough
　形 徹底的な；詳細な
☐ expiration date
　有効［消費；賞味］期限
☐ quality management
　品質管理
☐ proprietary
　形 所有者の；商標で守られた
☐ hygiene management
　衛星管理

What other kinds of things do you eat raw?

ほかにもどんなものを生で食べますか？

In addition to fish, we also eat horsemeat, beef, and chicken raw.

魚のほか、馬肉、牛肉、鶏肉なども生で食べます。

It is said that *sashimi* was born because Japan is an island nation, making fish easy to get.

日本は島国なので、新鮮な魚が手に入りやすいため刺身が生まれたと言われています。

The fact that the cutting quality of knives in Japan is high thanks to its sword technology may also be a reason.

日本刀の技術を生かした切れ味のいい包丁があることも一因かもしれません。

食文化

205

THEME 80 どんぶりの使用
Use of *Donburi*

 80

庶民の食生活には必要不可欠な食器それはどんぶり。ごはん食文化を語るうえでも欠かせないこの器を実際の料理とともにご案内しては？

ここにもやっぱり生卵！　夏場以外でご提案しましょう

英語で言うと？

歴史がある：**have a history (of)**　ごはんとおかず：**rice and side dishes**　こどもから大人まで：**people of all ages**　丸い：**circular**　四角い：**square**

Photo: ガイムさんによる写真 AC からの写真

Why are "donburi," or bowls, used so commonly?
どんぶりの使用が多いのはなぜ？

● Because *donburi* hold lots of rice, a staple in Japan.

どんぶりは日本人の主食であるごはんがたくさん入るからです。

● The use of *donburi* also has a long history, having been used since the Muromachi period.

日本は室町時代からこれを使っていたという古い歴史があります。

□ staple
名 主食；必需品

Because we can eat rice and side dishes from *donburi* quickly, which suits the busy Japanese lifestyle.

□ suit
動 合う；適合する

ごはんとおかずが手早く食べられるため、どんぶりは忙しい日本人の生活に合っているからです。

What are some popular *donburi* dishes in Japan?
日本で人気のどんぶりメニューは？

"Oyakodon," which consists of chicken, onion, and egg, is popular with people of all ages.

□ consist of
〜から成る

鶏肉、玉ねぎ、卵が入った親子丼は、子どもから大人まで人気です。

"Gyudon," which consists of beef and onion and has a sweet, spicy flavor, is also commonly eaten.

牛肉と玉ねぎを甘辛く味付けした牛丼もよく食べます。

"Tendon," which consists of shrimp and vegetable *tempura* on a bed of rice, has been a favorite since the Edo period.

海老や野菜の天ぷらがごはんに乗った天丼は、江戸時代から愛されています。

What is the difference between *donburi* and "ojuu"?
どんぶりとお重の違いは？

Donburi is a circular container, while *ojuu* is a square container.

□ circular
形 円の；丸い
□ container
名 容器

どんぶりは丸い器で、お重は四角い器です。

Most *donburi* are earthenware, while most *ojuu* are lacquerware.

どんぶりは陶製、お重は漆製のものが多いです。

There are also *donburi* and *ojuu* made from paper and plastic so they can be taken home.

持ち帰り用に、紙やプラスチックなどでできたものもあります。

食文化

THEME 81

ホットスナック（コンビニレジ横の食べ物）
Hot Snacks (foods near convenience store registers)

コンビニのホットスナックは、チェーンごとに工夫が凝らされていてクオリティが高いです。寒い季節にはおでんの食べ比べもおすすめ！

コンビニおでんは冬のホットスナック代表格！

英語で言うと？

食べ比べする：**try and compare**　人気を誇る：**boast popularity**　肉まん：**steamed meat bun**　定番：**standard**　伝統的な：**traditional**　練り製品：**foods made from fish paste**

Photo: amadank / PIXTA（ピクスタ）

What is a "hot snack?"
ホットスナックってなんですか？

It refers to warm finger food sold near the registers primarily at convenience stores.

おもにコンビニのレジ横で売られている温かい軽食のことです。

Generally, fried chicken, croquettes, and French fries prepared at each store are sold.

一般的に、それぞれの店舗で調理された、唐揚げやコロッケ、フライドポテトなどが販売されています

□ ffinger food
　指でつまんで食べられる軽食

□ croquette
　名 コロッケ

208

🍙 They're popular because people can eat freshly made food.

できたてが食べられるので人気です。

How should I enjoy them?

どのように楽しんだらいいですか？

🍙 Each convenience store chain has their own new products, so it's recommended that you try and compare them.

コンビニのチェーンごとに独自の新商品も出ているので、食べ比べるのもおすすめです。

🍙 Items made using chicken boast the highest popularity at every convenience store.

チキン系のメニューは、各コンビニで首位の人気を誇っています。

☐ boast
動 ～を誇ってい

🍙 In cold seasons, steamed meat buns are a winter standard as they are easy to eat and warm us up.

寒い季節には肉まんで手軽に体を温めるのが、冬の定番です。

☐ bun 名 丸いパン

Are there also Japanese foods?

日本食もありますか？

🍙 "Oden," a traditional Japanese food, is also a hot snack.

伝統的な日本食の「おでん」もホットスナックのひとつです。

🍙 It consists of vegetables and foods made from fish paste boiled in stock.

野菜や練り製品をだし汁で煮込んだものです。

🍙 We can select the items we want, put them in a cup that's provided, and pay for them at the register.

決められたカップに、自分で選んだ食材を入れ、レジでお金を払います。

B級グルメ
B-Class Gourmet

旅先の味を体験するのも旅の醍醐味。Ｂ級グルメは得てして家庭でも再現できるものがあるので、簡単なレシピ説明もできるといいかも。

英語で言うと？

庶民的：**for ordinary people**　安い：**inexpensive**　ご当地ならではの：**local specialty**　たこ焼き：**octopus dumplings**　お好み焼き：**savory pancakes**　日本各地：**throughout Japan**

Photo: Naokam さんによる写真 AC からの写真

What is "B-class gourmet?"
Ｂ級グルメってなんですか？

It is cooking that, despite being inexpensive and for ordinary people, is delicious. It refers to enjoying eating that kind of cooking.

安くて庶民的なのに美味しい料理。また、そのような料理を好んで食べることを言います。

☐ ordinary people
一般大衆

There is B-class gourmet that is unique to regions throughout Japan.

日本全国に、その地域ならではの「B級グルメ」が存在します。

 There are many types of B-class gourmet, from Japanese to western cuisine.

☐ cuisine　名 料理法

和食から洋食まで、さまざまな種類のB級グルメがあります。

 What are the popular dishes in B-class gourmet?

人気のB級グルメにはどんなものがありますか？

 As recipes that can easily be made at home, we have "yakisoba," or fried noodles, "takoyaki," or octopus dumplings, and "okonomiyaki," or savory pancakes.

☐ dumpling
名 ダンプリング；餃子
☐ savory
形 いい味のする

家庭で簡単に作れるものとして、焼きそばやたこ焼き、お好み焼きがあります。

 Dishes like curried rice, omelette rice, and rice balls are also popular.

カレーライスやオムライス、おにぎりなども人気です。

 Dishes like "ton katsu," or pork cutlet, "gyudon," or beef bowl, and hamburg are eaten in every region of Japan.

☐ hamburg
名 ハンバーグ

とんかつや牛丼、ハンバーグなども日本各地で食べられます。

 Are there also sweets?

スイーツもありますか？

 There are also sweet B-class gourmet dishes, such as "taiyaki," or fish-shaped cakes filled with bean jam, pancakes, and "anpan," or bread rolls filled with red bean paste.

☐ bean jam　あんこ
☐ red bean paste
　あんこ

たい焼きやパンケーキ、あんぱんなど、スイーツ系のB級グルメもあります。

食
文
化

😊 Recently, shaved ice and pancakes made from glutinous rice flour are also popular.

最近ではかき氷や、もち米の粉で作ったパンケーキも人気です。

😊 The selection of sweets at convenience stores has expanded, and it might be interesting to take a look.

コンビニのスイーツが充実しているので、のぞいてみると面白いでしょう。

☐ shaved ice
かき氷
☐ glutinous
形 粘りのある

富士宮やきそば。2006年に行われたB級ご当地グルメの祭典「B-1グランプリ」で初代王者に輝いた

THEME 83

精進料理
Vegetarian Cooking

 83

ベジタリアンが多い訪日観光客のご案内には、精進料理の知識は欠かせません。宿坊体験の情報なども、調べておくと喜ばれます。

長野の宿坊にて提供された精進料理

食文化

英語で言うと？

動物性たんぱく質：**animal protein** 修行僧：**monk** 低カロリー：**low in calories**
高たんぱく：**high in protein** 無駄：**waste** 思想：**philosophy**

Photo: Licensed under Public Domain via Wikimedia Commons / Flickr 帰属：Chris 73

What is vegetarian cooking?
精進料理って何ですか？

It is cooking that uses seasonal ingredients from the four seasons without using animal protein such as meat or fish.

□ protein
名 タンパク質

肉や魚などの動物性たんぱく質を使わず、四季折々の旬の食材で調理する料理です。

213

In the 6th century, it came to Japan from China along with Buddhism.

6世紀に、仏教とともに中国から日本に伝わりました。

It was originally for meals for monks.

□ monk　名 僧侶

もともとは修行僧のための食事でした。

Is vegetarian cooking attracting attention?
精進料理が注目されているのですか？

Yes, as it is low in calories and high in protein, making it suitable for dieting.

□ suitable for
　　〜に向いている
□ dieting
　　名 食事療法すること

低カロリー・高タンパクなため、ダイエットに適しているからです。

It is also a cooking method characterized by the fullest use of the ingredients to avoid waste.

食材を生かしきり、無駄が出ないようにする調理法にも特徴があります。

It is prepared completely by hand, without using microwave ovens or semi-prepared foods.

電子レンジや半調理品などを使わず、すべて手作業で行います。

Is there any impact from Zen philosophy behind vegetarian cooking?
精進料理の背景には、禅の思想が影響しているのですか？

The foundation of the philosophy of vegetarian cooking was built by the Dogen who founded the Soto sect in the early Kamakura period.

□ philosophy
　　名 哲学

□ sect　名 派閥

精進料理の理念の基礎を築いたのは、鎌倉時代初期に曹洞宗を興した道元です。

The Dogen, who believed that "daily life is all training," preached that "cooking and eating are also part of training."

道元は「日常生活のすべてが修行」とし、「食事を作ることも食べることも修行のうち」と説きました。

□ preach
動 （人に）説教する

If you consider that the food you eat today is the you of tomorrow, you will naturally take food more seriously each day.

今の食事が未来の自分をつくると思うと、自然と毎日の食事を大切するようになります。

食文化

これがなければ精進料理は成立しないと言っても過言ではない、大豆＆大豆食品。これらおなじみの食材以外に、肉としか見えない＆思えないような料理も数多く作られている

Photo: kai / PIXTA (ピクスタ)

THEME 84 外食文化
Dining-Out Culture

短期旅行の場合は特に、食事はほとんどが外食になります。日本人が普段使いする外食文化ってどんなの？ときかれることも多いです！

多くの日本人の「外食」の原体験はこれ！お子様ランチ！

英語で言うと？

お手頃価格の：**reasonably priced**　外食する：**dine out**　小鉢：**small bowl**　お得な：**good value**　庶民：**ordinary person**　居酒屋：**Japanese-style pub**

Photo: サカパさんによる写真 AC からの写真

What kinds of foods can we enjoy when dining out in Japan?

日本で楽しめる外食にはどんなものがありますか？

From reasonably priced beef bowl chain stores to fancy French cuisine, you can enjoy many types of food when dining out.

リーズナブルな牛丼チェーン店から高級フレンチまで、さまざまなタイプの外食を楽しむことができます。

□ dine out　外食する

◉ Lunch sets in particular are priced lower than dinnertime meals, and they come with small bowls, so they're a good deal.

とくにランチセットはディナータイムより価格が安く、小鉢などもついてお得です。

◉ *Izakaya*, or Japanese-style pubs, are recommended for enjoying common Japanese foods at reasonable prices.

庶民的な和食をリーズナブルに楽しむには居酒屋がおすすめです。

 What kinds of places do most Japanese people dine at?

日本人はどんなところで外食することが多いですか？

◉ On a daily basis, most people dine at fast food shops or diners.

日常的にはファストフード店や定食屋などです。

□ on a daily basis
　毎日の（ように）
□ diner
　名 軽食レストラン

◉ When enjoying dinner with friends or coworkers, we go to *izakaya* or family restaurants.

友人や同僚たちと夜ご飯を楽しむときは、居酒屋やファミリーレストランへ行きます。

□ coworker　名 同僚

◉ When celebrating occasions such as anniversaries or farewells, we make reservations at fancy restaurants.

記念日や歓送迎会などのときは、予約をして高級レストランへ行きます。

□ farewell
　名 送別会

食
文
化

THEME 85

立ち食い、立ち飲み
Stand-Up Dining [Drinking]

昔から営業している立ち飲み屋に加え、一見さんでも入りやすい新しい立ち飲み・立ち食い店も増えています。しかもジャンルもいろいろ！

東京は吉祥寺の超人気居酒屋、いせや総本店！焼き鳥がうまい！

英語で言うと？

配給制：**ration system**　酒類：**alcoholic beverages**　ピークを迎える：**approach the peak**　立ち食い店：**stand-up restaurant**　（店などが）狭い：**small (shop, etc.)**　詰める：**make space for**

When were there first stand-up drinking shops in Japan?

日本では、いつから立ち飲みのお店があるのですか？

Since the Edo period, we have been able to purchase alcohol at a liquor store and drink it right there while standing.

酒屋の店頭で酒を購入し、その場で立ったまま飲むことは、江戸時代から行われていました。

In 1943, the number of types of alcohol temporarily decreased due to a rationing system, and it became legal again in 1949.

1943年に酒類が配給制になると一時消滅し、1949年に合法的に再開しました。

□ decrease 動 減る
□ rationing system
　配給制度
□ legal 形 合法の

After that, stand-up drinking peaked in the 1960s, and then went out of fashion once the high-growth period came around.

その後、立ち飲みは1960年代にピークを迎え、高度成長期になるとすたれていきました。

□ go out of fashion
　流行遅れになる
□ high-growth
　period
　高度成長期

Are stand-up dining shops common in Japan?
立ち食いのお店は、日本では一般的なのですか？

Most common in Japan are stand-up *soba* shops. They sold things such as alcohol, *sushi*, and *tempura* since the Edo period.

日本で最も一般的なのは立ち食い蕎麦屋です。江戸時代から酒や寿司、天ぷらなどが売られていました。

□ stand-up
　立って行う

Additionally, there are culinary offerings such as *yakitori* and curried rice which don't take too much time to prepare.

そのほか、焼き鳥やカレーライスなど、調理に時間のかからない料理が提供されています。

□ additionally
　副 さらに

Recently, restaurant chains have emerged serving dishes that take longer to prepare, such as French cuisine and steak.

最近ではフランス料理やステーキなど、調理に時間がかかる料理を提供するチェーン店も出てきました。

□ restaurant chain
　レストランのチェーン店

As most shops have limited space, once the shop becomes crowded, you should make space for the new customers.

スペースの小さなお店が多いので、お店が混んできたら、新しいお客にスペースを譲りましょう。

食
文
化

角打ち（かくうち）
Kakuuchi (combined liquor store and bar)

 86

飲食店ではなく、酒屋で買ったお酒をその場で飲むというスタイルも、新鮮な日本体験！　地元のお客さんとのコミュニケーションも魅力！

英語で言うと？

酒屋：**liquor store**　安価で：**affordable**　升：**wooden cup**　静かなブーム：**quiet resurgence in popularity**　おつまみ：**snacks**　自家製の：**homemade**

Photo: AmbientNOK / PIXTA (ピクスタ)

What is "kakuuchi"?
角打ちとはなんですか？

It means to drink alcohol bought at a liquor store either inside the store or out front. It also refers to shops where you can do that.

酒屋の店内や店先で、その酒屋で買った酒を飲むこと。また、それができる酒屋のことです。

There are also cases where stand-up bars you can enjoy for lower prices are called *kakuuchi*.

安価で楽しめる立ち飲み屋のことをそう称する場合もあります。

🙂 *Kakuchi* is also used to refer to the style of drinking where you place your lips against the corner of a square *masu*, or wooden cup.

四角い升の角に口をつけて飲むこと行為を、「角打ち」と呼ぶこともあります。

Where did *kakuuchi* start?

角打ちはどこで始まったのですか？

🙂 It is said that *kakuuchi* started in the Kitakyushu region.

角打ちは北九州地域で始まったとされています。

🙂 Workers drinking alcohol at a liquor store on the way home from work came to be referred to as *kakuuchi*.

労働者が仕事帰りに酒屋で酒を飲んでいたことが「角打ち」として定着しました。

🙂 After that, workers moved to all areas of Japan, and it is said that this is how *kakuuchi* culture spread.

その後労働者が全国各地に移動し、文化が広がったと言われています。

Are there shops even today where we can enjoy *kakuuchi*?

現在でも角打ちできるお店はあるのですか？

🙂 In Japan, *kakuuchi* is enjoying a quiet resurgence in popularity.

日本では、角打ちが静かなブームとなっています。

☐ resurgence
名 復興；復活

🙂 Towns which, until now, had not operated *kakuuchi* establishments, are beginning a modern-day *kakuuchi* one after another.

これまで角打ち営業をしていなかった街の酒屋が、続々と現代風の角打ちを始めています。

☐ establishment
名 設立
☐ modern-day
現代の

THEME 87

せんべろ
Senbero (inexpensive place to drink)

こちらも庶民派の飲み方、せんべろ。一ヵ所でダラダラと長居するのではなく、サッと飲んでパッとつまんで店を出るのが「粋」なのです。

昔懐かしい雰囲気は今や貴重

英語で言うと？ -

とても安い：**extremely low price** 　リピーター：**repeat visitor** 　べろべろになる：**very drunk** 　社交場：**social gathering place** 　お通し：**appetizer** 　はしご酒：**barhopping**

 ## What is "senbero"?
せんべろとは何ですか？

It means a bar with extremely low prices, where you can drink alcohol to your heart's content for only 1,000 yen. It also refers to drinking at such a place.

☐ to one's heart's content
思う存分

1000円も出せばべろべろになるほど酒が飲める、料金が非常に安い酒場のこと。また、そのような酒場で飲むことです。

222

◉ In fact, it is used to mean a snack plus two or three drinks for 1,000 yen.

実際には1000円でおつまみとお酒2〜3杯飲めるという意味合いで使われます。

◉ According to the book, *Senbero Tantei ga Iku*, the custom has spread nationwide.

書籍『せんべろ探偵が行く』によって、全国に広がったと言われています。

 Why is "senbero" popular?
なぜ、「せんべろ」が人気なのですか？

◉ Because the number of shops that are "delicious though inexpensive and have a great atmosphere" has increased.

安くてうまく、雰囲気がいいお店が増えたためです。

☐ atmosphere
名 雰囲気

◉ There are more and more shops where repeat visitors are increasing due to the quality of the cooking and the comfort level.

料理のクオリティーと居心地のよさで、リピーターを増やすお店が増えています。

☐ comfort
名 心地よさ

◉ The fact is that there isn't anyone who gets completely drunk; it's a social gathering place where people enjoy alcohol in a stylish way.

実際にべろべろになるほど飲む人はおらず、スマートにお酒が楽しめる社交場となっています。

☐ gathering place
集会所

Where and how can we enjoy *senbero*?

せんべろはどこで、どのように楽しめますか？

● While there are *senbero* spots nationwide, the ones in Tokyo around Akabane, Ueno, and Tateishi are well known.

日本全国にせんべろスポットがありますが、東京ではとくに赤羽・上野・立石あたりが有名です。

● Most of the shops don't have appetizers, so you can drink just a little and then move to a different shop.

お通しがない店が多いので、少し飲んで、すぐ別のお店に移動することができます。

□ appetizer
名 前菜

● While barhopping is really enjoyable, we have to be careful not to overdo it.

はしご酒はとても楽しいですが、飲みすぎないように注意が必要です。

□ barhop
動 はしご酒する
□ overdo
動 ～をやりすぎる

せんべろの"聖地"、
赤羽！

Photo: まちゃー / PIXTA（ピクスタ）

224

おせちの由来・込められた意味
The Origin of and Meaning Incorporated in *Osechi*

お正月には必須のおせち料理、縁起のいい料理が重箱にギッシリ詰め込まれています。「マメに…」「よろコンブ」などの解説もしましょう

1段目：祝い肴・2段目：焼き物（海産物中心）・3段目：煮物（野菜中心）

英語で言うと？

伝統的な：**traditional**　お供えする：**offering to the gods**　主婦：**housewife**
家事：**chore**　解放する：**free**　保存のきく：**cured**

Photo: asphoto / PIXTA（ピクスタ）

食文化

Is *osechi ryori* eaten in Japan during *oshogatsu*?

日本ではお正月におせち料理を食べるのですか？

Osechi ryori is traditional Japanese cooking specially prepared for *oshogatsu*, or New Year's.

おせち料理は、特別に準備されたお正月のための伝統的な和食です。

Oshogatsu is a special event celebrated during the first week of the year.

正月は、1年の最初の週を祝う特別なイベントです。

□ celebrate 動 祝う

 Special *oshogatsu* cooking, *osechi*, is prepared by the end of December.

12月の終わりまでに、特別な正月料理「おせち」を準備します。

What is the origin of *osechi*?
おせちの由来はなんですか？

 Originally, foods that were eaten while offered to the gods was called "osechiku."

本来は、神様にお供えして食べるものを「御節供（おせちく）」と呼んでいました。

 In the Edo period, dishes prepared for *oshogatsu* began to be called "osechi ryori."

江戸時代には、お正月にふるまう料理を「おせち料理」と呼ぶようになりました。

 The gods would rest in the "kamado," or cooking stove, and to free housewives from having to do chores, ingredients that could be saved were primarily used.

かまどの神様に休んでもらい、主婦を家事から解放するため、保存のきく食材が中心になりました。

□ cooking stove
料理用コンロ
□ free
動 ～を自由にする
□ chore
名 雑事；作業

Please tell me about the meaning behind *osechi*.
おせちに込められた思いを教えて下さい。

 Osechi ryori is placed in a square box called "jyuubako."

おせち料理は、「重箱（じゅうばこ）」と呼ばれる四角い箱に詰めます。

🍵 Appetizers are placed in the highest box, the second box contains primarily seafood, and the third box holds mountain delicacies.

１番上の箱には、酒の肴（さかな）を、２番目には、海の幸を中心に、３段目には山の幸を中心に入れます。

🍵 *Kuromame*, or black beans, represent the ability to live a healthy life on beans, and *renkon*, or lotus root, allows you to see the future. Each ingredient holds a different meaning.

黒豆はマメで元気に暮らせるように、レンコンには、将来の見通しがきくように……など食材にもそれぞれ願いが込めれています。

□ delicacy
名 ごちそう

□ represent
動 ～を表す；象徴する

□ ability
名 才能；能力

□ lotus root
レンコン

食文化

世界一の門松としてギネスに認定もされた、長崎県の橘神社の巨大門松！

Photo: kattyan / PIXTA (ピクスタ)

THEME 89
地域の食文化
Regional Food Culture

同じ日本国内でも気候や地形が異なるように、その土地の「味」も全然違います。その魅力というか基本情報を解説してみましょう。

西の昆布だし、東の鰹だし！

英語で言うと？

南北にわたって：**extending north to south**　暑い [寒い] 地方：**warm [cold] region**　土地の特徴：**characteristics of the land**　だし：**soup stock**　昆布：**kelp**　かつお：**bonito**

Photo: jazzman / PIXTA (ピクスタ)

Photo: jazzman / PIXTA (ピクスタ)

Are there differences in food culture from one region to another in Japan?
日本では、地域ごとに食文化に違いがあるのですか？

Japan is a long island extending north to south, and in each region original food culture was born.

日本は南北に長いので、各地域で独自の食文化が生まれました。

Each region's food culture reflects the characteristics of its land - from warm and cold regions to those facing the sea and those enveloped in mountains.

暑い地方と寒い地方、海に面した地域や山に囲まれた地域など、その土地の特徴が食文化にも反映しています。

□ envelop
動 ～を包む

Even domestically, there are completely different customs in Japan, and you'd be surprised.

日本国内でも、全く異なる風習があることがあり、驚くことがあります。

Are there also differences between eastern and western Japan?

関東や関西にも違いはあるのですか？

In eastern Japan, colors are vivid and they use strong, dark soy sauce, while in western Japan colors are more subtle and they use a refined, light soy sauce.

関東は色が濃く旨味もしっかりした濃口しょうゆを使い、関西は色が薄く味わいも上品な薄口しょうゆを使います。

□ subtle 形 繊細な
□ refined 形 上品な

There are also differences in the ingredients for soup stock. In western Japan they make stock quickly from "konbu," or kelp, while in eastern Japan they use "katsuo," or bonito, and spend more time making it.

「だし」の原料にも違いがあります。関西は「昆布」で短時間でだしをとり、関東は「かつお」でじっくりだしをとります。

□ kelp 名 昆布
□ bonito 名 カツオ

Looking at sandwich bread, they prefer the crisp, eight-slice loaf, while in western Japan the chewy, 4-slice loaf is popular.

食パンでは、関東ではパリッとした8枚切り、関西はもっちりした4枚切りが人気です。

□ loaf
名 (パンの) ローフ
★切っていない塊の状態
□ chewy
形 腰の強い

Are there also differences in the composition of meals from one region to another?

食事の内容にも、地域ごとの違いがあるのですか？

Popular *okonomiyaki* and *takoyaki* in the Kansai region are sometimes eaten as side dishes with white rice. These are not eaten as side dishes in the Kanto region.

関西で人気のお好み焼きやたこ焼きは、「おかず」として白いごはんと一緒に食べることがあります。関東では、それらをおかずにはしません。

In Kagawa Prefecture, which is famous for *udon*, it is customary to eat *udon* from a bathtub upon the construction of a new home. The wish is to live an intense, long life.

うどんで有名な香川県では、家を新築したとき、湯船でうどんを食べる風習があります。「太く長く生きられるように」の願いが込められています。

In Nagano Prefecture, when serving tea to guests, they serve pickles, instead of bean-paste buns or rice crackers, as refreshments.

長野県では、お客様にお茶を出すとき、お茶うけとしてお饅頭やお煎餅ではなく、漬物を添えます。

☐ composition
名 組み立て

☐ customary
形 普通の；習慣の
☐ intense
形 非常に強い

☐ refreshment
名 (元気回復させる)
飲食物；(複数形で)
軽食

Photo: kikisorasido / PIXTA (ピクスタ)

Chapter 4

外国人がいちばん不思議に思う

日本の娯楽・建造物・宿泊

　最後は、雑談にも大いに役立つ 11 のネタ。競艇や競輪などの公営競技は、できれば実際にレースを見て迫力を感じたいものです。また、カプセルホテルは値段もさることながら、非日常感が味わえて人気があるようです！

AMUSEMENT
BUILDING
ACCOMMODATION

THEME 90 競艇
Speedboats

選手の駆け引きが見どころの競艇（BOAT RACE）。ギャンブル初級者で
も入りやすく、フリードリンクやWi-Fi完備の会場も多い

「水上の格闘技」とも表現される競艇。生で見ると迫力満点！

英語で言うと？

人工的な：**manmade**　駆け引き：**negotiation**　格付けされる：**be ranked**　優勝
賞金：**prize money**　予想屋：**handicapper**　解説：**breakdown**

Where can I watch speedboat racing?
競艇はどこで見ることができるのですか？

You can watch it at a special venue for speedboat racing.

競艇を行うための専用の場所で見ることができます。

☐ speedboat racing

There are 24 of them in Japan.

日本には24箇所存在します。

As well as the ocean and lakes, there are also courses with manmade lakes.

海や湖などのほかにも人工的に水面を作ったコースがあります。

□ manmade
形 人工の

What kind of race is it?
どんな競技ですか？

Six boats compete in a race.

6艇でレースを競います。

It's a 1,800 meter race in which they complete three laps of a 600 meter course.

600mのコースを3周する1800mの競技です。

The races are divided into ranks, and the higher the rank, the higher the prize money.

レースは格付けされていて、格が高いほど優勝賞金が高くなります。

How do people like to watch it?
どんな楽しみ方がありますか？

There are people called "yosouya" (tipsters), who will give you a breakdown of the race and likely winner for about 100 yen.

予想屋と呼ばれる人がいて、だいたい100円ぐらいでレースの解説や買い目を教えてくれたりします。

□ tipster 名 予想屋
□ breakdown
名 分析結果

There are also venues that will let fans on the boat with the competitors.

ファンサービスで選手とボートに乗れる会場もあります。

□ competitor
名 競争相手

Racers who are young, handsome men, and female racers are popular.

若手のイケメンレーサーや女性のレーサーも人気を集めています。

競輪
Keirin

91

競輪・競艇・オートレースと並んで公営競技の1つである競輪。レースは
ほぼ毎日開催されており入場料も安いので、気軽に見に行ってはどう？

選手たちが乗っている自転車の重量は約7〜8kg

英語で言うと？

競走路：**race track**　予想：**prediction**　投票する：**post**　フルオーダー：
completely made-to-order　地面との摩擦：**friction with the ground**　先導車：
leader

Photo: takuzero / PIXTA (ピクスタ)

What kind of race is *keirin*?

競輪とはどんな競技ですか？

● People ride bicycles on a course and
compete to reach the finish line first.

競走路上を自転車で走り、誰が一番最初にゴールするかを競い
ます。

● It's not just a contest of speed, but also
overtaking opponents.

スピードだけでなく、相手との駆け引きが見どころです。

□ overtaking
名 追い越し
□ opponent
名 対戦相手

😊 You can write your predictions on a mark card, or post them on the internet.

自分の予想をマークシートに記入するか、ネットから投票します。

□ prediction
名 予想

What kind of bicycles are used?
どんな自転車が使われますか？

😊 They are completely made-to-order for the athletes.

選手のために作られた完全オーダーメードのものです。

□ made-to-order
オーダーメイドの

😊 The bicycles are built for speed, so they don't have brakes.

スピードを出すことを追い求めた自転車なので、ブレーキがありません。

😊 They have thinner tires than normal bicycles to reduce friction with the ground.

地面との摩擦を減らすために、普通の自転車よりも細いタイヤが使われます。

□ reduce　動 減らす
□ friction　名 摩擦

Is it the same as the Olympic event called *keirin*?
オリンピックの正式種目である Keirn と一緒ですか？

😊 It was created in Japan, but general races have slightly different rules to the Olympic event.

発祥は日本ですが、一般のレースとオリンピックの競技では少しルールが違います。

□ slightly
副 わずかに

😊 In Olympic keirin, there is a leader called a "pacer" who sets the pace for the race.

Keirin には「ペーサー」と呼ばれるレースのペースを作る先導車がいます。

😊 Blocks that are allowed in Japanese *keirin* are banned at the Olympics.

競輪で許されているブロックは禁止されています。

□ block
名 ブロック；阻止

THEME 92
ロト
LOTO

92

ロトとは購入者が数字を選択する形式の宝くじ＝数字選択式全国自治宝くじの一つ。ほかにもナンバーズ、ビンゴなど全5種類ある。

英語で言うと？

数字選択式：**number-selection method** 　宝くじ：**lottery** 　キャリーオーバー：**carryover** 　当せん金額：**prize money**

Photo: こてっちゃん / PIXTA (ピクスタ)

What's LOTO?
LOTOってなんですか？

🧑 It's the name for a kind of lottery based on choosing numbers that is sold in Japan.

日本で発売される、数字選択式の宝くじの名称です。

🧑 You can buy a ticket at a lottery counter, from some bank ATMs and online.

宝くじ売り場や一部の銀行のATM、またネットでも購入できます。

□ lottery 名 くじ

□ ATM (=automatic telling machine) 現金自動預払機

There is a carry-over system so if you don't win first prize or you have money left over, it will be carried over to the next first prize.

□ carry-over 次に
持ち越される

１等当選が出なかった場合や、配当金が余った場合は次回の１等配当金に繰り越される、キャリーオーバーというシステムがあります。

What types are there?
どんな種類があるの？

There's LOTO 7, where you choose seven different numbers from one to 37, LOTO 6, where you choose six different numbers from one to 43, and Mini LOTO where you choose five different numbers from one to 31.

１～37の数字の中から異なる７個の数字を選ぶロト７、１～43の数字の中から異なる６個の数字を選ぶロト６、そして１～３１の数字の中から異なる５個の数字を選ぶミニロトがあります。

LOTO 7 is 300 yen per ticket, LOTO 6 and Mini LOTO are 200 yen per ticket.

ロト７は１口300円、ロト６とミニロトは１口200円です。

The prize money for each one is different, up to 600 million yen for LOTO 7, up to 200 million yen for LOTO 6, and about 10 million yen for Mini LOTO.

当せん金額は、１等がそれぞれ、ロト７は最高６億円、ロト６は最高２億円、ミニロトは約1,000万円です。

娯楽

パチンコ
Pachinko

 93

漫画やアニメ、映画、お笑い芸人やミュージシャンなどとタイアップされた遊技機もたくさんあるので、面白がる訪日観光客も多いのでは？

英語で言うと？ -

大当たり：**jackpot**　　パチンコ玉：**pachinko ball**　　景品交換する：**prize exchange**
丸いハンドル：**round handle**　　右回り：**clockwise**　　ドル箱：**cash cow**

Photo: bee / PIXTA (ピクスタ)

What's *pachinko*?
パチンコって何ですか？

It's a kind of game where you roll little metal balls down a glass-covered board, and try to get them into prize holes.

ガラスに覆われた盤面上で小さな鉄の玉を転がし、入賞口に入れて当たりを狙う娯楽です。

If you get a ball into a jackpot hole, more balls will come out, but if you miss, you'll gradually run out of balls.

大当たりすれば玉は出ますが、はずれると手持ちがどんどん減っていきます。

At the end you can exchange however many balls you have left for a prize.

最終的に残った玉の数に応じて、景品交換をします。

How do I play it?
どうやって打つの？

First, you rent balls at a *pachinko* parlor.

まずはパチンコ店内で玉を借ります。

At the bottom right of the *pachinko* machine is a round handle which you turn to the right and aim for the prize holes.

パチンコ台の右下に、丸いハンドルが付いているので、右回りに回して入賞口を狙います。

The further right you turn the handle, the more force is put into the balls.

右側に回せば回すほど、玉は勢いよく飛びます。

Is there any etiquette?
マナーはありますか？

You mustn't hit the *pachinko* machine.

パチンコ台を叩いてはいけません。

If you leave your seat, you leave something of yours or the ball tray there.

席を離れるときは、持ち物やドル箱（玉の入った箱）を置いておきます。

If you are going to take a long break, say something to the staff.

無断で長い休憩をとるときは店員にひと言かけましょう。

□ jackpot
名 賞金；特賞
□ run out of
〜を使い果たす

娯楽

239

ティックトック
TikTok

 94

世界で人気のTIKTOKは、訪日するお客様の中にはすでに動画を作っている人もいるかも！　基礎知識ぐらいはもっておくほうが無難かも。

英語で言うと？

動画：**video**　爆発的人気の：**super popular**　投稿する：**upload**　動画撮影する：**take a video**　特殊効果：**special effect**　□パクする：**lipsync**

Photo: iStockphoto.com / Wachiwit

What's TikTok?
TikTok ってなんですか？

It's a video app that was created in China, and has become super popular among young people in Japan too.

中国で生まれた動画のアプリで、日本の若い子の間でも爆発的な人気を呼びました。

□ app　名 アプリ

🙂 It's a platform where you can make short videos, from 15 seconds to one minute long, and upload them.

□ upload
動 アップロードする

15秒から１分ほどの短い動画を作成、投稿できるプラットフォームです。

🙂 When you take a video, you can adjust the speed to film at 0.5 speed, or 2x speed, and use special effects that are in the app, so it's popular because anyone can easily make a funny video.

動画を撮影する際に「0.5倍速」「２倍速」と、速さを調節しながら撮影をしたり、アプリ内の特殊効果を使って誰でも簡単に面白い動画が作れるため人気を呼びました。

What does everyone do on there?
みんなどんなことをしているの？

🙂 Videos of dancing along with background music, posing, and lipsyncing are popular.

□ lipsync
動 口パクで歌う

BGMに合わせて踊ったり、ポーズをとったり、口パクをする動画が人気です。

🙂 People post videos of themselves doing popular dances in groups. Some people watch the videos of popular users and post their own versions.

流行ったダンスをみんなでマネして投稿します。人気ユーザの動画を見て自分のオリジナルを加えて投稿したりします。

🙂 People who use TikTok are called TikTokers, and there are TikTokers with many followers who become popular.

□ follower
名 ファン；フォロワー

TikTokをする人はTikTokerと呼ばれ、多くのフォロワーを持つカリスマ的な人気を集めるTikTokerもいます。

THEME 95 ボウリング場
Bowling Alleys

⬇95

ボウリングは日本固有のものではありませんが、ゲーセンやカラオケ、ゴルフやバドミントンなど、一度に色々遊べる複合施設は喜ばれるかも。

英語で言うと？ --

～と併設する：**establish together with**　複合施設：**multi-use facility**
シニア層：**elderly people**　娯楽：**pastime**

Photo: トモヤ / PIXTA (ピクスタ)

Is bowling popular in Japan?
日本でボウリングは人気がありますか？

💬 Yes, there was a bowling boom in the 1970s and it spread throughout the country.

はい、1970年代に爆発的なボウリングブームがあり全国に広まりました。

242

😊 Currently, there are bowling alleys in complexes with *karaoke* facilities, so it's popular with young people.

現在はカラオケなども併設された複合施設にもボウリング場があるため、若者にも人気があります。

😊 Bowling is also a popular pastime among elderly people who experienced the bowling boom.

かつてのボウリングブームを経験したシニア層にもボウリングは人気の娯楽の一つです。

What kind of place are bowling alley complexes?

ボウリング場の複合施設はどんな場所ですか？

😊 Facilities that include *karaoke*, a game center, sticker printing machines, and restaurants are popular.

カラオケやゲームセンター、プリントシール機、飲食店などが充実している施設が人気です。

😊 There are also large facilities where you can try all kinds of sports like badminton, golf and basketball.

バドミントンやゴルフ、バスケなどのあらゆるスポーツが体験できる大型施設もあります。

😊 Some facilities are open from morning until dawn the next day, but minors usually need to be accompanied by a guardian, depending on the time.

朝から夜明けまで営業している施設もありますが、たいてい未成年は時間によっては保護者の同伴が必要になります。

娯
楽

THEME 96
古民家、リノベ
Kominka and Renovations

 96

古い住居に価値を見出す欧米のお客様や、伝統的なものに強く惹かれるリピーター勢などは特に、こういう少しマニアックなネタに興味深々です。

英語で言うと？

建築方法：**construction method**　民家：**private home**　柱：**pillar**　梁：**beam**
接合部：**joint**　水回り：**plumbing**　町家：**townhouse**

Photo: takapon / PIXTA (ピクスタ)

 What kind of building is a "kominka"?
古民家とはどんな建物ですか？

It's a house built with traditional Japanese methods.

日本の伝統的な方法で建てられた民家です。

It usually refers to houses more than 50 years old.

通常、築50年以上のものをさします。

244

Most of them don't use metal for pillars and beams.

柱や梁の接合部分は金物を使わない建物が多いです。

□ pillar 名 柱
□ beam 名 はり

 Why are they appealing?
どんな魅力がありますか？

 Because we can enjoy old buildings that you don't see these days.

今ではみられない昔ながらの建築を楽しめます。

 The older they are, the more history they have.

年月を重ねた分、歴史をがあります。

 By renovating them, we can create a unique atmosphere combining old and new.

リノベーションをすることで、古い良さと新しさが他にはない雰囲気を生み出します。

□ renovate
　動 修理［改修］する
□ combine
　動 ～混ぜ合わせる

 How are the buildings used after renovation?
リノベーションしてどんな風に利用されるのですか？

 Plumbing and other facilites are added, and they are used again as housing or offices.

水回りなどの設備を整えて、再度住居や事務所として使用されたりします。

□ renovation
　名 修復；刷新

 Some of them are used for cafes like coffee shops, or art galleries, making use of the old-fashioned house atmosphere.

古民家の雰囲気を活かして、喫茶店などの飲食店、ギャラリーなどにも利用されます。

 There are also popular *ryokan* that are made from renovated Kyoto townhouses.

京都の町家をリノベーションした人気の旅館もあります。

□ townhouse
　名 都市住宅

工業地帯
Industrial Zones

非日常感を味わえる工業地帯は、日本人にもファンが多いですが、観光地ではないので、クルーズやツアーをおすすめするようにしましょう。

川崎の工業地帯の夜景

英語で言うと？

非現実的な：**surreal**　風景：**scenery**　独特の：**unique**　夜景：**night view**　石油化学コンビナート：**petrochemical complex**　密集して：**densely**

Photo: lupin0333 さんによる写真 AC からの写真

Why are industrial zones so popular?
どうして工業地帯が人気なんですか？

There are many people who are fascinated by the surreal, science fiction movie-like scenery of industrial areas.

工業地帯の持つ非現実的でSF映画のような風景に魅せられる人がたくさんいます。

☐ industrial zone
　工業地帯
☐ fascinate
　動 ～を魅了する
☐ surreal
　形 非現実的な
☐ scenery　名 景色

246

The unique atmosphere of the night view is also gaining popularity.

また、その夜景の持つ独特の雰囲気も人気を集めています。

There are people who visit industrial areas as a hobby, and bus tours that go around industrial areas are also popular.

趣味で工業地帯を訪れる人や、工業地帯を見て回るバスツアーなども組まれて人気があります。

Where are the popular night view spots?
人気の夜景スポットはどこですか？

There's a petrochemical complex that was built in Yokkaichi in the 1980s. A night view cruise looking at it from the sea is popular.

四日市の昭和30年代に大規模形成された石油化学コンビナート。海からみる夜景クルーズが人気です。

□ petrochemical complex 石油化学コンビナート
□ cruise
名 クルージング

The Keihin Industrial Zone, which has been developed in the Kawasaki Seaside area, is densely populated with factories, and many plants light up for work at night. There are a lot of tours to see this night view.

川崎臨海部に展開する京浜工業地帯は工場が密集していて、夜には多くのプラントに作業用の明かりが灯ります。 この夜景を見るツアーもたくさんあります。

□ densely
副 密集して
□ populate
動 居住させる

Also,Muroran in Hokkaido is famous in the north, and Kitakyushu's industrial area in the south.

他にも北は北海道の室蘭、南は北九州の工業地帯も有名です。

建
造
物

タワー
Towers

98

建造物でいえば、高いタワーも人気のスポットです。初めて訪れる土地では、最初に展望台から全体を見渡してみるのもおすすめです。

東京スカイツリー。隣接する東京ソラマチには水族館やプラネタリウムも

英語で言うと？

〜のシンボル的な：**a symbol of 〜**　電波塔：**radio tower**　ライトアップする：**light up**　展望塔：**observation tower**　商業タワー：**commercial tower**　高層階：**the top floor**

写真提供：(公財) 東京観光財団

What kind of building is Tokyo Tower?
東京タワーってどんな建物ですか？

It's a 333 meter radio tower that is a symbol of Tokyo.

東京のシンボル的なタワーで、333メートルの電波塔です。

It lights up at night. The light changes to various patterns to match events.

夜にはライトアップされます。ライトアップはイベントに合わせて色んなパターンに変化します。

◉ There's a "Tower Shrine" in Tokyo Tower.

東京タワーには「タワー大神宮」があります。

 What other towers are there?

他にはどんなタワーがありますか？

◉ Osaka has an observation tower called Tsutenkaku, which is a symbol of Osaka, and a popular tourist spot.

□ observation
tower　展望塔

大阪には通天閣という展望塔があり、大阪のシンボルであり、人気の観光スポットです。

◉ In Kyoto, there is Kyoto Tower in front of Kyoto Station.

京都には京都駅前に京都タワーがあります。

◉ A new symbol of Tokyo is the 634m commercial tower called the Skytree.

□ commercial
tower
商業用タワー

東京には新たなシンボルとしてスカイツリーという634m の商業タワーがあります。

 How do I experience them?

それぞれの楽しみ方を教えてください。

◉ There is a restaurant on the top floor of Skytree where you can dine while enjoying the view.

スカイツリーの高層階にはレストランがあり、展望を楽しみながら食事ができます。

◉ People say that if you touch the "Billiken" statue on the 5th floor of Tsutenkaku in Osaka, you will be happy.

大阪の通天閣の５F にある、「ビリケン」という像を触ると幸せになると言われています。

◉ At Kyoto Tower, you can experience making Japanese sweets.

京都タワーでは、和菓子作りなどを体験することができます。

建
造
物

カプセルホテル
Capsule Hotels

99

終電を逃したサラリーマンのみならず、欧米からの観光客や女性の需要が増加し、設備面やセキュリティ面の強化など、近年進化しています。

英語で言うと？

簡易ベッド：**cot**　2段：**split-level**　設置する：**install**　鍵をかける：**lock**　貴重品：**valuables**　コインロッカー：**coin-operated locker**

Photo: CAN CAN / PIXTA（ピクスタ）

What sort of hotel is a capsule hotel?
カプセルホテルとはどんなホテルですか？

A capsule hotel is a unique Japanese accommodation facility that provides a simple bed.

カプセル状の簡易ベッドを提供する日本独特の宿泊施設です。

Many of them are built alongside saunas.

サウナが併設されてることが多いです。

□ alongside
副 横に；そばに

250

🙂 Recently there are split level ones that two people can use.

最近では 2 段構造のものもあり、 2 人で利用することもできます。

What's it like in the bed?
ベッドの中はどうなってますか？

🙂 Generally there's only space for one adult.

大抵大人 1 人入るスペースしかありません。

🙂 There is lighting and a small television installed.

照明や小型のテレビが設置されてます。

🙂 You can't lock the capsule, so valuables are stored in a locker.

鍵をかけることができないので、貴重品はコインロッカーに預けます。

What sort of people use them?
どんな人が利用するのですか？

🙂 In the past, they were often used by businessmen who had missed the last train.

昔は終電を逃した会社員などが多く利用していました。

🙂 Now there are more stylish capsule hotels, and the number of female guests is increasing.

おしゃれなカプセルホテルも増えて、女性の利用客も増えています。

🙂 They're cheap so students and people who want to travel cheaply also use them often.

安価なので、学生や安く旅行したい旅行者も多く利用します。

宿
泊

民泊
Rental accommodations

100

宿泊に関しては、事前に下調べしてくる旅行者がほとんどと思われますが、雑談でこういったネタが出てくることは十分考えられますね！

英語で言うと？

民泊施設：**private accommodation** 〜へ届け出る：**apply to** 一軒家：**detached house** 一般家庭：**ordinary family** 農家：**farming household** 漁師：**fisherman**

Are rental accommodations popular in Japan?
日本で民泊は盛んですか？

Rental accommodation facilities in Japan have increased since the residential rental accommodation law was enacted on June 15th, 2018.

住宅宿泊事業法（民泊新法）が2018年6月15日施行されてから日本でも民泊施設が増えています。

☐ rental 形 賃貸の
☐ accommodation 名 宿泊施設
☐ residential 形 居住の

 The number of tourists increased so there was a shortage of accommodation facilities like hotels, and rental accommodations attracted attention.

訪日客が増えたことで、ホテルなどの宿泊施設が不足し、民泊が注目されるようになりました。

□ shortage 名 不足

□ attract attention 注目を集める

 You need to apply to the government to operate an accommodation facility.

民泊施設の営業を行うには、国への届け出が必要です。

 What types are there?
どんな種類がありますか？

 You can rent an entire stand-alone house, or a room like an apartment.

一軒家丸ごとやマンションなどの部屋を借りるこができます。

 There are also homestay types in which you stay with a regular family.

一般家庭に滞在するホームステイ型も存在します。

□ regular family 普通の家族

 There are also accommodation facilities where you stay in a farming household or with a fisherman, and experience things different to everyday life.

農家や漁師の家庭に滞在し、非日常を体験できる宿泊施設もあります。

□ farming household 農家

 How do I use one?
利用するにはどうすればいいですか？

 You can find websites for searching rental accommodation on the Internet.

民泊先を検索できるサイトなどをネットで探すことができます。

 You can also download an app for booking rental accommodation and make a reservation through the app.

また、民泊の予約ができるアプリなどをダウンロードすればアプリで予約することができます。

□ book 動 予約する

宿泊

●著者紹介

デイビッド・セイン　David A. Thayne

米国生まれ。証券会社勤務後に来日。日本での35年にわたる英語指導の実績をいかし、英語学習書、教材、Webコンテンツの制作を手掛ける。累計400万部を超える著書を刊行、多くがベストセラーとなっている。NHKレギュラー出演の他、日経・朝日・毎日新聞等に連載。著書に『ゼロからスタート英語を読むトレーニングBOOK』、『ゼロからスタート英語で話すトレーニングBOOK』（共著）、『デイビッド・セイン先生と英語で日本全国47都道府県めぐり』（すべてJリサーチ出版）ほか多数。企業・学校等でビジネス英語、TOEIC、日本文化を英語で紹介する講演会やセミナーも開催。AtoZ English 主宰。https://www.atozenglish.jp

本書へのご意見・ご感想は下記URLまでお寄せください。
https://www.jresearch.co.jp/contact/

カバーデザイン	喜田里子
本文デザイン・DTP	江口うり子（アレピエ）
本文イラスト	K.M.S.P. / PIXTA（ピクスタ）／田中斉
ナレーション	Jennifer Okano／Howard Colefield／Dominic Allen

英語でガイド！
外国人がいちばん不思議に思う　日本のくらし

令和元年（2019年）12月10日　初版第1刷発行

著　者	デイビッド・セイン
発行人	福田富与
発行所	有限会社　Jリサーチ出版
	〒166-0002　東京都杉並区高円寺北2-29-14-705
	電話03(6808)8801（代）FAX 03(5364)5310　編集部03(6808)8806
	URL https://www.jresearch.co.jp
印刷所	㈱シナノ パブリッシング プレス